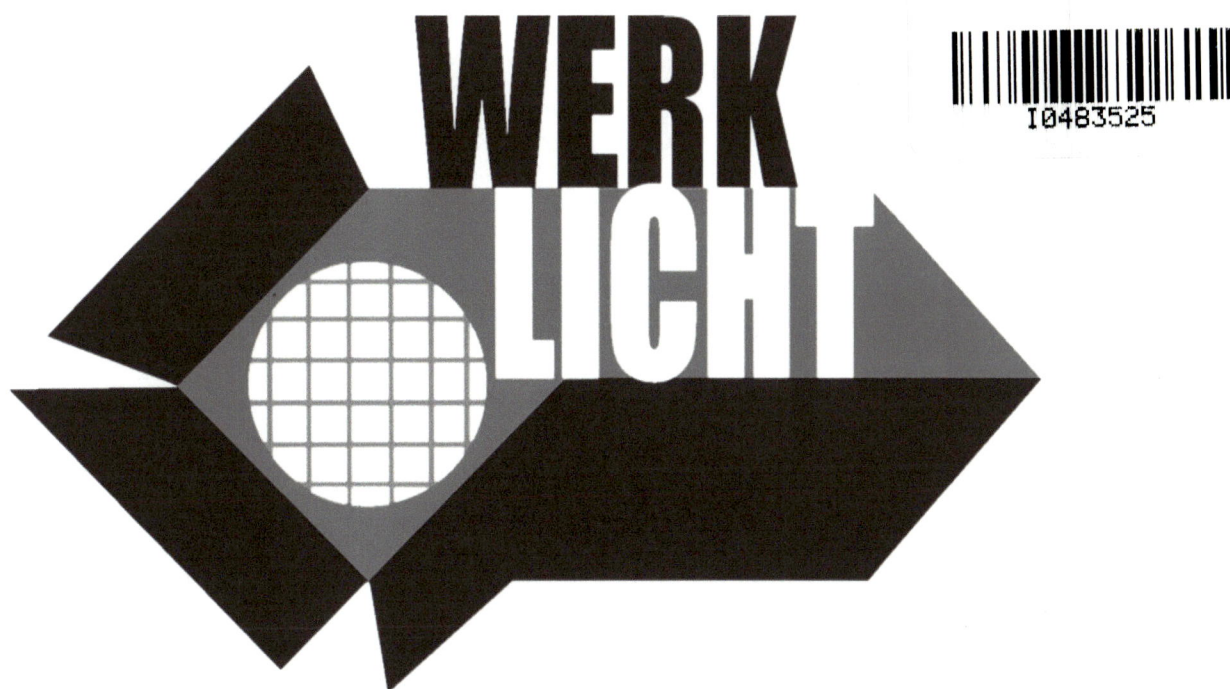

Werklicht Exposé

NL

Werklicht Exposé is met nadruk een expositieruimte; wij tónen werk. Kunstenaars krijgen, onafhankelijk van hun CV, de kans om hun werk te laten zien in een wijk waar kunst niet vanzelfsprekend is.
Iedereen kan binnenlopen voor een babbeltje en een kop koffie. De kunstenaars zijn zoveel mogelijk aanwezig tijdens de openingstijden van de expositie. Ontmoeting staat centraal; wij geloven dat we op die manier kunst toegankelijk en bereikbaar kunnen maken, zonder inhoudelijke concessies te doen.
Exposé is onderdeel van Werklicht, een sociaal-culturele stichting met multi-disciplinair karakter. Waar mogelijk zoeken we de combinatie met andere disciplines op; vaak zijn er concerten, poëzie-optredens of andere randprogramma's.

EN

Werklicht Exposé is an exhibition space, not a gallery. We show works. Artists do not have to show us their resume, they show us (and the neighbourhood) their works.
Everyone can swing by our space to have a chat and a coffee, meet the artist and see their art. Artists are, if possible, present during opening hours.
Meeting is a central value, because we believe that this is the way to make art accessible and available, without having to compromise.
Exposé is part of Werklicht, a social-cultural foundation with a multi-disciplinairy focus. Most of our exhibitions also have a side programme, for example a poetry reading or a mini-concert. We try to mix things up as much as possible.

Contact details:
www.werklicht.eu
info@werklicht.eu
06 58985480

Realities of War
dedicated to Wilfred Batty 1899-1981

Spades represent the dullness, mud, weariness and sordidness. Clubs stand for another side, the humour, the cheerfulness, the jollity, and good-fellowship. In diamonds I see the glitter of excitement and adventure. Hearts are a tragic suit of agony, horror and death. And to each man the invisible dealer gives a succession of cards

(Nothing of Importance: A Record of Eight Months at the Front (1917), Bernard Adams)

Introduction

Simon O'Corra trained as a theatre designer at the Mountview Academy, London in the mid 1980s and worked as a set and costume designer in London for some years. After this he worked as a multi-media arts facilitator with Action Space London Events, supporting and enabling people with a wide range of abilities and ages, to access their creativity. During this period Simon also began a series of oil paintings entitled '*Constraint*' on the subject of society's control of individuals by fashion. particularly focussing on corsetry.

A change of career focussing on social activism, advocacy, research and healing meant that Simon was away from painting for some years and has only in the last two years begun to create once more. He uses his experience in activism in his art, as a means to encourage the viewer to engage with well established events in different ways and to face up to an alternative reality. He has decided to create a **pentad** of projects to commemorate and examine the centenary of World War One, the first in this sequence being his book **'Life Goes On'**, (2013), a pictorial history of normal life and events using original *cartes postales*.

The second project in this pentad, a collection of paintings and collage work, entitled '*Realities of War*', presents the physical horrors endured by soldiers in the Great War (1914-1918) by combining painting with contemporary *cartes postales* and advertising from magazines. This series also has a personal focus for Simon, as it is inspired by a story told to him when he was six years old by his grandfather Wilfred. This began by him disclosing the fact that his brother had been killed at the Battle of the Somme and having been pushed to talk more by the young boy, Wilfred spoke with tears in his eyes about witnessing the decapitation of his best friend at the same battle. He had never ever been able to shake that image from his mind and suffered regular nightmares even after four decades. Simon is able to pinpoint the development of his fatalist / realist view of the world and particularly of war, to this one happening when he had found someone who was willing at last to tell the truth about an event and not pull their punches in the description of it. He has such respect for his grandfather because he bared his soul to him that one time and this has made Simon the man he is today.

It is difficult to underestimate the impact that propaganda had upon the masses in history's first modern war, which saw the mobilization and regimentation of entire societies to an unprecedented degree. World War One was a 'total war 'for its European participants, and that totality was made possible in large measure due to the creation of an equally modern propaganda as revealed in these postcards or cartes postales. The effectiveness of this propaganda in hardening the utter distinction between 'us' and 'them' is seen in the aftermath of the war in the harshness of terms dictated to Germany in the Treaty of Versailles. It was this harshness and heavy-handed vengeance towards the German people that led directly to the rise of Adolf Hitler and the Nazi Party, and ultimately the Second World War.

(http://www.ww1-propaganda-cards.com/home.html)

These realities of war, were terrifying for all concerned, with their blood, guts and gore which the groups interested in developing medical and chemical experiments and mechanised war, fed upon like hungry vultures. This axis advanced their agenda with blind nationalism, overt prejudice and a sense of self righteous revenge. Capitalists were at the heart of the war, and their insidious propaganda which both encouraged the growth of a fraternal and nationalistic code and and at the same time seduced people into seeking consolation in whatever they wanted to sell, covered every angle and spoke to all: men, women and children. They skillfully juxtaposed, in their marketing campaigns, bombs and bullets with beauty and luxury which engendered a loss of innocence recognised by populations, but only when it was too late, which clearly then had led to an overwhelmingly cynical view about the absurdity of the negotiated peace.

It is now a common place view in left-wing circles that wars are started to satisfy capitalist interests; arms manufacturers and the like and there is no reason to refute that assertion in terms of the First World War. Thus the current Socialist Party of Great Britain declares that -

What was responsible for these wars was the whole world system of capitalism with its competitive struggle for profits and its collection of competing armed states. (http://www.economist.com/blogs/buttonwood/2014/08/first-world-war-and-capitalism)

Yet it has been also said, in opposition to this, that the Great War was brought about by aristocratic communities with their abhorrence of Trade who were in their last triumphant twilight before they too would be swept away by the very war they may have created but, unlike the Capitalists, not profited from. If in reality Capitalism was not the originator of the War it did along with its individual members use the conflict to its own advantage and to great effect, even perhaps prolonging the combat for its own ends. Was it not they who encouraged the use of propaganda and persuasive psychological marketing methods to encourage everyone to do their bit and continue to do so until the bitter, and it was a harrowing and empty, end?

Picking up the Pieces

The surgeon Harold Gillies describes the sight, following the Somme, of 'men burned and maimed to the condition of animals'. A prosthetic mask could never replicate the warmth and expressive range of a human face, but it could hide the 'dreadful abyss' of raw being and restore a semblance of humanity. Biernhoff, Susannah, The Rhetrorc of Disfigurement in First World War Britain, Ocford University Press 2011.

The fact that over 11,000 operations were performed on some 5,000 servicemen between 1917 and 1925 can hardly be reckoned with given the human suffering that was involved in this newest of medical procedures occasioned by and developed because of the newly mechanised warfare of WW1 and its ability to mutilate and obliterate the very humanness of its protagonists.

Hideous is the only word for these smashed faces: the socket with some twisted, moist slit, with a lash or two adhering feebly, which is all that is traceable of the forfeited eye; the skewed mouth which sometimes—in spite of brilliant dentistry contrivances—results from the loss of a segment of jaw; and worse, far the worst, the incredibly brutalising effects which are the consequence of wounds in the nose, and which reach a climax of mournful grotesquerie when the nose is missing altogether.

(Muir, Ward., The Happy Hospital, 1918)

At face value these paintings appear naturalistic and even one-dimensional, but if one studies the symbols contained within each piece they reveal cynical, sarcastic and mocking characteristics, like those found in contemporary magazines such as the *Wipers Times*, published by the soldiers themselves at the Western Front. They knew only too well the reality of war and wrote biting and caustic jokes, as only they were then entitled to, about the horrible environments and callous butchery they were experiencing. These works also express the 'ever present pointlessness of war', for the ordinary man and woman. Populations were, over the four years of the war, completely decimated. The only people truly benefiting from the world's wars are the arms dealers and equipment suppliers and those seeking to control populations through such activities as money lending and politics.

The Paintings - pages 8 - 29.

1. **Heart of my Friend** - Thrusting lads, emboldened by propaganda, proud of themselves, close to one another, handsome and well turned out. They are friends, brothers, comrades. They share a closeness that death has ripped apart and yet their love remains even if the survivor is reticent about delving into the new reality of his friend. This is the heart of his missing friend he is approaching, seeking, in that bloody cavity, the memories they shared. He was unable to help his friend at the end but he can now honour the heart of his friend with a memory touch. *'The Heart of my Friend'* explores the old pals network fostered by the British Government of the time to entice through peer pressure, large groups of young men who all knew each other and were even from the same village to join up to fight for King and country. *Cartes postales* (postcards) produced at the time, often depicted a close fraternal bond between the lads, bolstered by an apparent certainty that they were doing the right thing to fight for freedom. However, many villages and towns were devastated by the determination of Field Marshall by Haig and Co. to lead their lambs to slaughter.

2. **No More Words** - This work represents a person, full face on only half of it is missing. He is a non Western European, perhaps Bulgarian or Romanian. This shows a different war, fought in the Great Plains. The people at the bottom right are perhaps prisoners of war. Some men had to live with this kind of horror for the rest of their lives in an era without plastic surgery and a still developing prosthetics industry. This man has a blank eye expression but a foreboding anger and sadness.

3. ***'Your Country Needs You'*** - A play on the old Lord Kitchener propaganda poster, this time showing the reality of that original poster's message. The mustard gas here creates a smokescreen and the blown away eye increases the man's confusion and prevents him from seeing what is really going on. The use of psychological conditioning previously used in advertising as early as 1895 in the United States, was now put to good effect in hoodwinking the masses into believing the war hype.

4. **Hole-y War** - This image plays with the irony and cynicism that was expressed by men at the Front in their printed journal *The Wipers Times*. These men were perfectly placed to comment accurately on the true horrors of wars, so often set in motion using religion and the moral high ground as arbiters for victory and sacrifice. The title is also a play on words, as this man has had part of his face blown away, creating a gaping hole revealing shattered teeth, therefore reducing the need for the 'toothpaste' in the advert behind him.

5. **A Working Chair Leg** - Many many men lost their limbs during the conflict, a devastating injury in itself and also a death knell for a man's employment and social future. Of course this destruction at the hands of this mechanised war also occasioned a need for false limbs, hence the advertisement and the lower right hand image of injured soldiers, one with a walking stick.

6 .The Frustrations Of The Gourmand - This depicts the medical experiments that mutilated soldiers who became human guinea pigs in this terrible conflict underwent. Having been a gourmand in every sense of the word before the war, the image of the soldier bearing tubed pedicles, gives a horrifying glimpse into this soldier's Great War experience and his post war years of suffering and pain. Such practices often took years to achieve good results.

7. The Hands That Caressed - How many young men lost their charm and their tenderness in this conflict, beaten out of them by the horror of the trenches and other battlegrounds and with it their ability to please another, to stroke a loved one or to hold their children at their births. This is witnessed in this painting, a soldier back in Civvy Street but without the capacity for a delicacy of touch or the ability to create with their hands. Their loved one, the dreamed of love of their life is a receding memory in this image, blood spattered like the rest of him.

8. Falling - This is inspired by the artist's grandfather's tale of the death of his best pal at the Battle of The Somme (1916), where he had his head blown clean off. He recounted this tale when he was six years old and it has formed his desire and readiness always to present things as they are. This particular image was based on a story heard in a TV documentary about a 'wounded soldiers' hospital where a nurse reported that someone, a Sikh soldier, came in with his skull blow open and brains falling out and yet the man was still alive. In depicting a Sikh, the aim was also to present the international nature of this particular conflict.

9. Grounding Props - As if painkillers could obliterate the damage done to the soldiers at the Front! Merchandise for pain was still being sold to the general populace and would have invariably been used by soldiers for the physical torment many would face. Of course the emotional and mental scars would endure and most often go undiagnosed and therefore untreated often for years to come. So alongside the analgesic, all a soldier could hope for as a prop for his fragile person would be the regulation set of crutches, these ones decorated with emblems from an arts journal of 1914.

10. Ruined Bodies - This convent with its body of nuns, is in abject ruination, grotesque and twisted and yet still recognizable. It echoes the reality for this soldier, cut through in his body and with his withered hand reflecting the damaged railings which once demarcated the convent grounds.

11. Elbowed Out - In the bigger picture of the war it is clear to see that so many young and older men were elbowed out of the world, figuratively and actually. A whole generation lost to their own future and that of the countries from whence they came. Shattered limbs for those who survived still meant that many were shoved aside, jostled to the boundaries of society, every bit as lost as if they had been killed in battle.

12. Badass Enemy - This image for the first time recognises the sacrifice made by the men of the United States. It's stark and provocative portrayal foretells of the way in which the New World ideas from the United States would influence Europe both as an ally and as a guiding Post-War cultural force.

13. Blind Side - Following on from Badass Enemy this image depicts an African American, suffering heavily from the burning effects of Mustard Gas, which was able both to blind a man but also to seep through his clothes and burn his body. He has a tube of anti-gas ointment tucked into his shorts, although it is unknown if this gave the men much solace

14. Exuding - Not only were men gassed and blinded by Mustard Gas used by the Germans in 1917 (although it was created by a Belgian by birth, Frenchman in 1822) but it also burned and blistered the skin, so even if you wore a mask the gas could penetrate clothing and wreak havoc on the skin. This gas along with others was a cynical development in Modern warfare and one which would pave the way for subsequent genocides by gas.

15. **Decimated Manhood** - As soldiers often had to sit in muddy conditions it was often the case that the mustard gas which sank into the quagmire would seep inside a man's trousers doing untold damage to his groin, his penis and his testicles. What was once a young man's pride and joy became an unspeakable burden, to be hidden away, another living death in a man's life.

16. **The Eyes Have It** - What if a photographic enthusiast had gone to the Front and lost his sight, indeed lost his eyes? How would that feel to him? How relevant would that bit of 'Verascope' advertising be to him, as it was so often the case for other men with different war wounds in adverts for other products.

17. **Sit Down, No Fuss** - Countless virile, sturdy young men came back from the Front so badly wounded as to need a wheelchair for the rest of their lives, with every part of what they had known before inaccessible to them, impossible to properly take part. The wheelchair was meant to give a measure of independence but back then it also served as a trap, a means to silence a man, who might say goodness knows what about what he had gone through. The wheelchair marginalised army men.

18. **Face Off, Face On** - A new kind of horror was seen in the First World War, one though which did not kill men but instead created a group in society who were the first to have prosthetic faces, to hide the decimation that their physiognomy had suffered. Paints were needed akin to make- up to match skin tones and enhance their ashen countenances.

19. **What Is The Point?** - This image is not about a 'seen' war wound. This is post war, something which a large amount of men ended up doing, as there was no recourse to support, understanding, work or a normal social and family life. This man needed to find a metaphor for his feelings of desperation and a harsh death in line with his past experience at the Front.

20. **No Choice Hero** - The final in the series is about the ultimate betrayal, a man who has returned from the Front, a hero, yet he is severely shell shocked and because of the embarrassment his behaviour evokes, he is incarcerated, locked away, and in effect, silenced. He feels he has no choice but to create the ultimate disappearing act in line with the way in which society has gagged him.

The Process - (a selection, pages 29 - 44)

A personal statement from the artist.

Often the inspiration for a painting stemmed from a particular *cartes postale* as in Number 1 ***Heart of My Friend***. This image touched me as being one of devotion between two friends, with arms around each other, optimistic and sure of themselves. This with hindsight made me feel sad as that sureness and confidence was as so often the case, misplaced. Whereas in other paintings it is the advertising images which suggest the irony of the soldier's situation as in Number 4, ***Hole-y War***, which features a man with a decimated face, blown away by a shell, leaving a gaping hole through his mouth, having destroyed teeth. The advertising is concerned with a toothpaste and shows nymph like creatures and a gently cascading waterfall, cleansing the pain perhaps. A further mode of working involved something read by myself or heard on a TV documentary as in Number 8, ***Falling,*** and focusses on a patient brought in still conscious with his brains clearly visible through a shattered skull. This image is an homage to the Sikh soldiers who were engaged in the War and who are so often forgotten, especially in subsequent atrocities instigated against them by the British in India.

So in these instances, pre-existing art/photography from the period 1914-1918 were used to develop ideas and then on to paper. These images suggested the overall look of each painting. Sometimes it was the number of soldiers in *cartes postales* that tied in with the feel of an image, as in Number 19, **What is the Point**, a scene of a suicide of an ex soldier having hurled himself from above onto a railing, the many spokes piercing his body and echoed in a *cartes postale* image of 4 soldiers in a row. Always the paintings began life as a blank sheet of paper with a *cartes postale* pasted onto the sheet in the approximately correct position. The overall image would then be drawn around this photograph with other advertising images added after the painting was well under way.

The process after the gluing of the *cartes postales* involved laying in of colours and fields and particularly at the boundary between the photographs and the original sheets, to attempt to mask the raised edges of the photos. After some time though I began to realise that I did not wish to hide the fact that buried in the painting was a *cartes postale* and that in order to be most effective there had to be some idea of its whereabouts.

All of these paintings are mounted onto old French oak planks, taken from a damaged building and framed by laths once used in an old barn.

The Sources - (a small selection, page 45 - 50)

The jagged fragment of a bursting shell will shear off a nose, an ear, or a part of a jaw, leaving the victim a permanent object of repulsion to others.
Biernhoff, Susannah, The Rhetrorc of Disfigurement in First World War Britain, Ocford University Press 2011.

The artist also used as inspiration, a range of contemporary images of equipment and clinical photographs of injury, disfigurement and treatments of the period.

In conclusion it is easy to imagine how and why many men with facial and body disfigurement fell foul of melancholy or suicide, when that which outlines a man's character and personality and also his status in the world is obliterated and what remains, is abhorrent to that man's culture and society.

Collaboration -

A specially commissioned musical composition by Matthew Holmes is being written to complement the series. The composer is working closely with the artist to marry the two creative mediums.

Simon O'Corra now lives, writes and paints in the South of France. www.lepuitsdelapaix.com

Special thanks to Nigel Bray of Sachet Mixte Publications for formatting and design of this book.

The PAINTINGS.

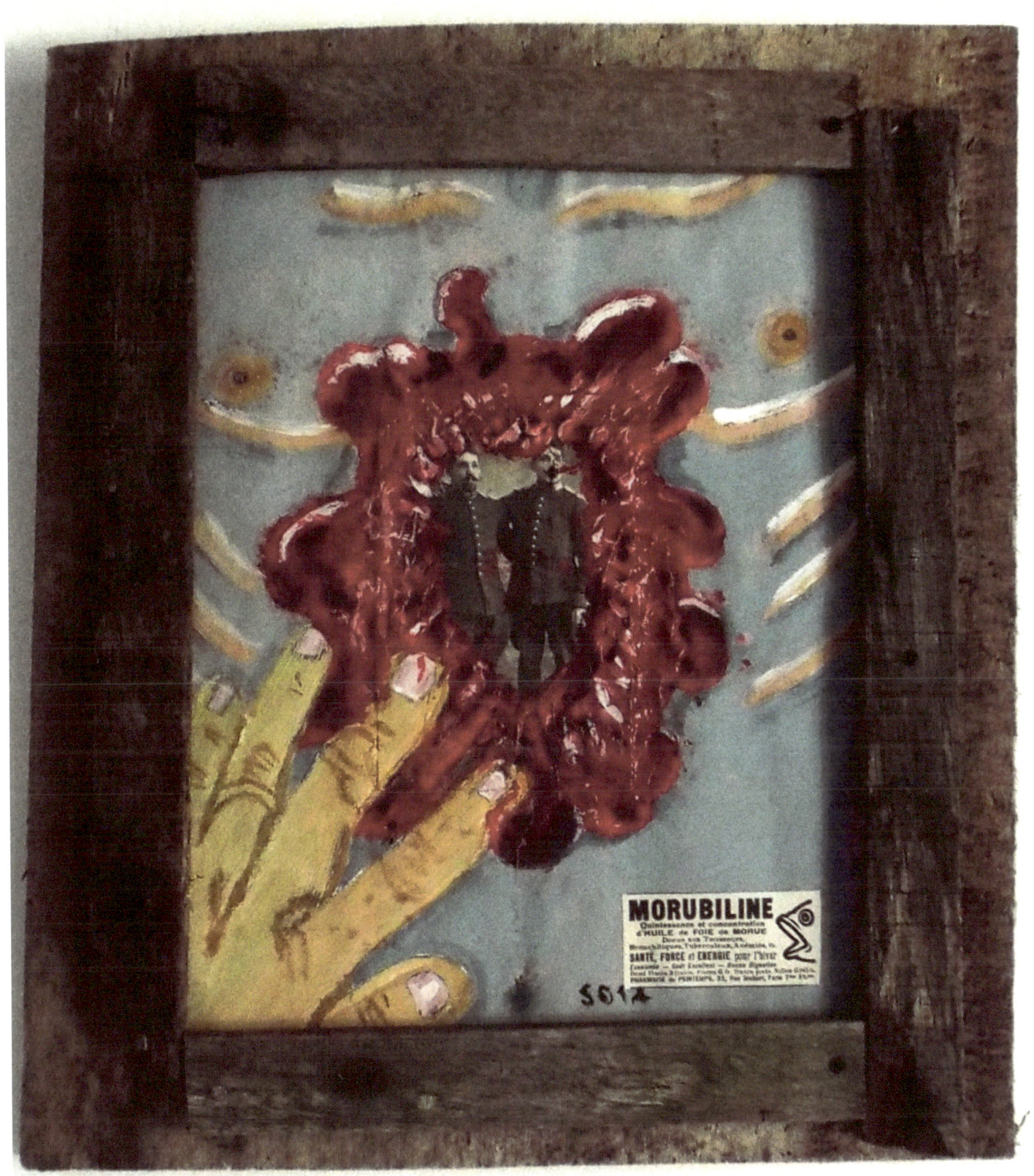

1. Heart Of My Friend.

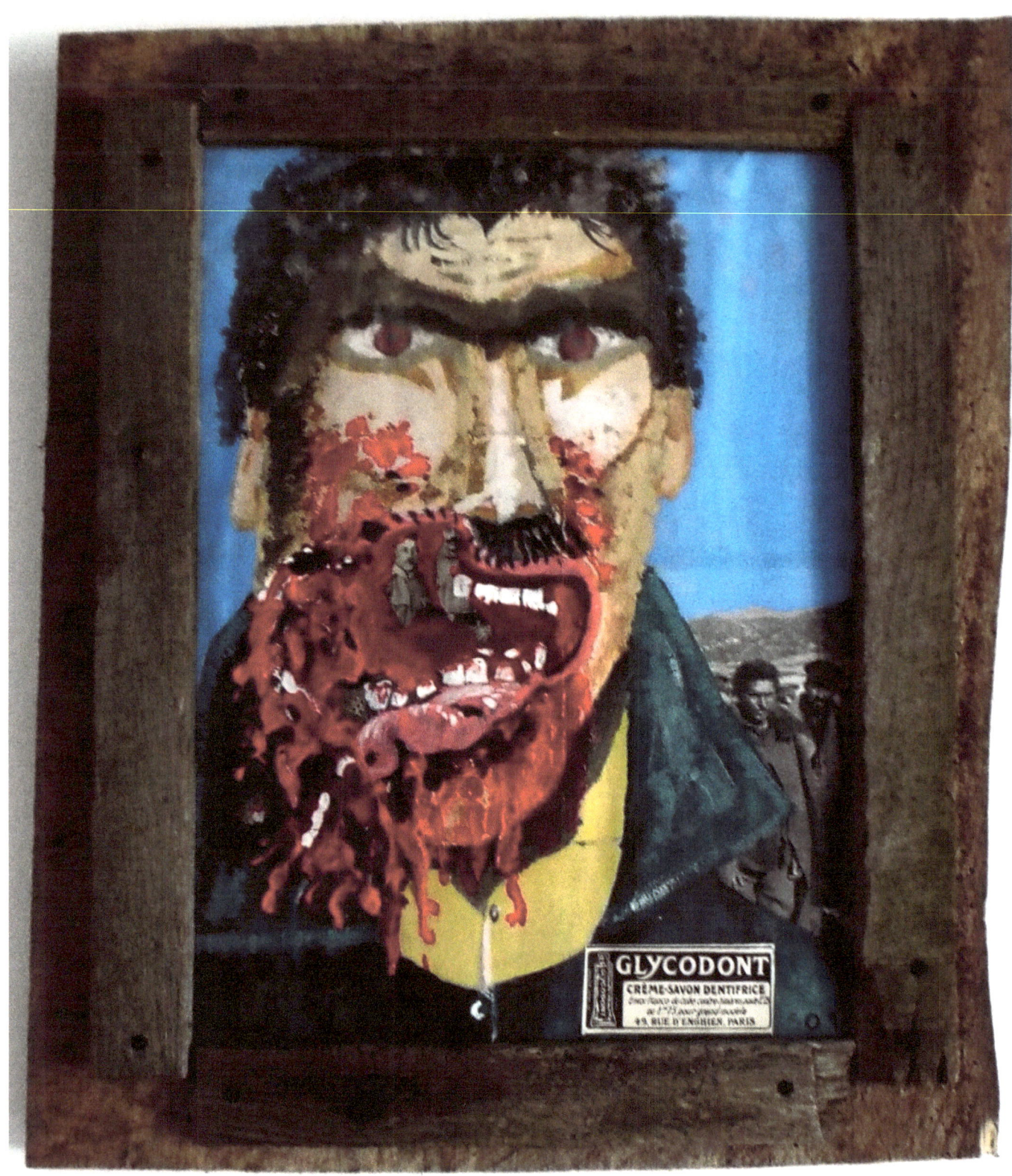

2. No More Words.

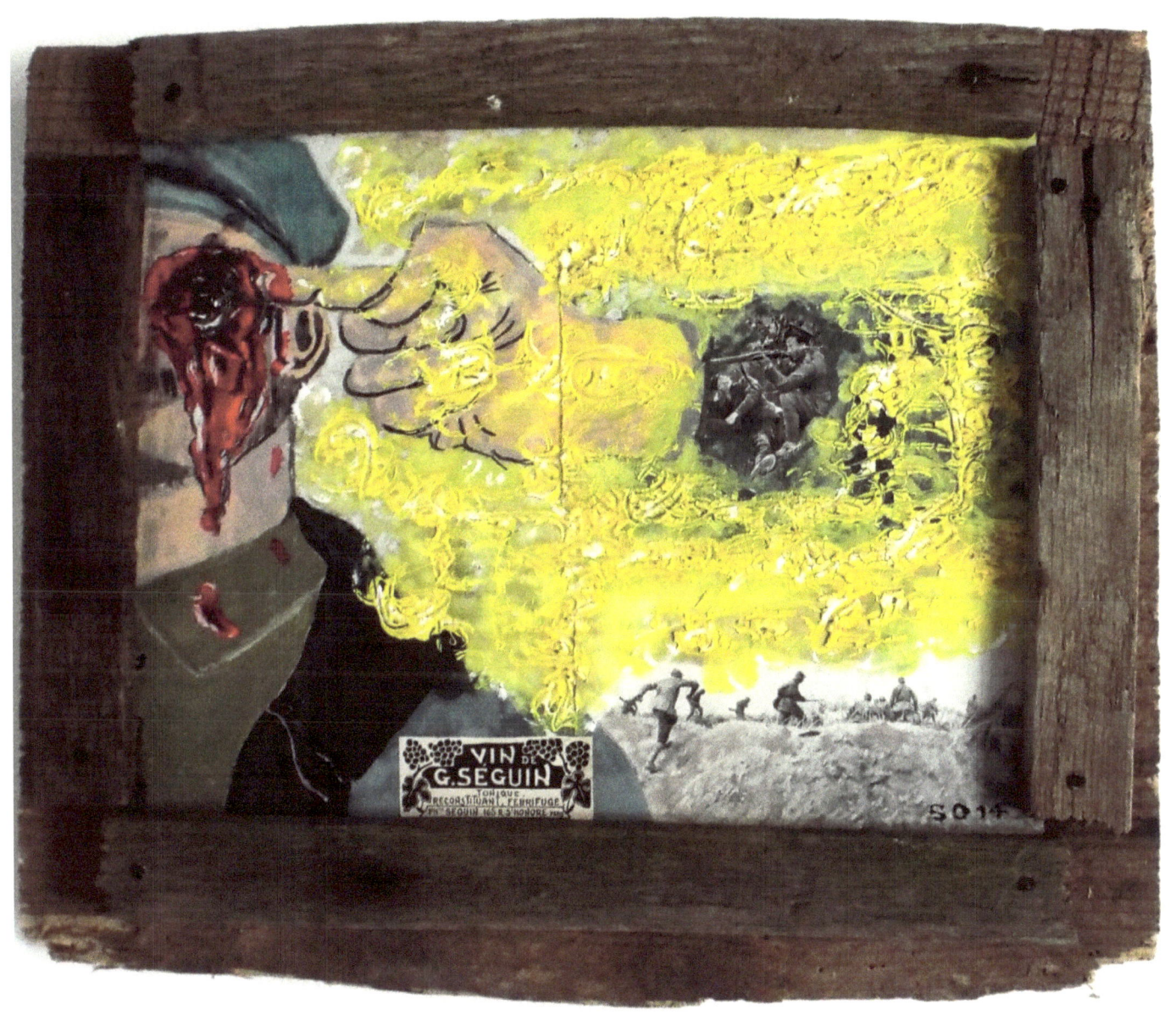

3. Your Country Needs You.

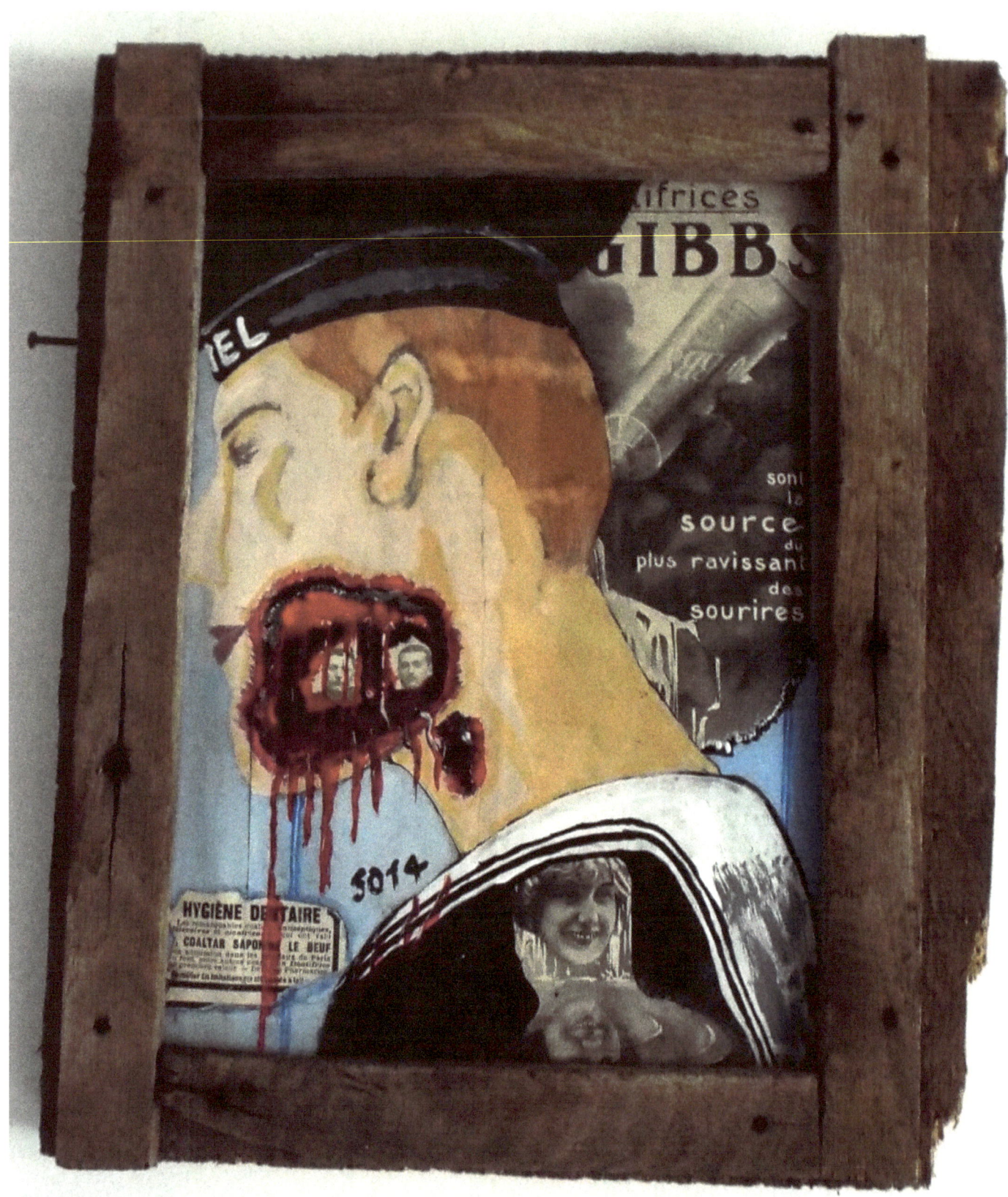

4. Hole - y War.

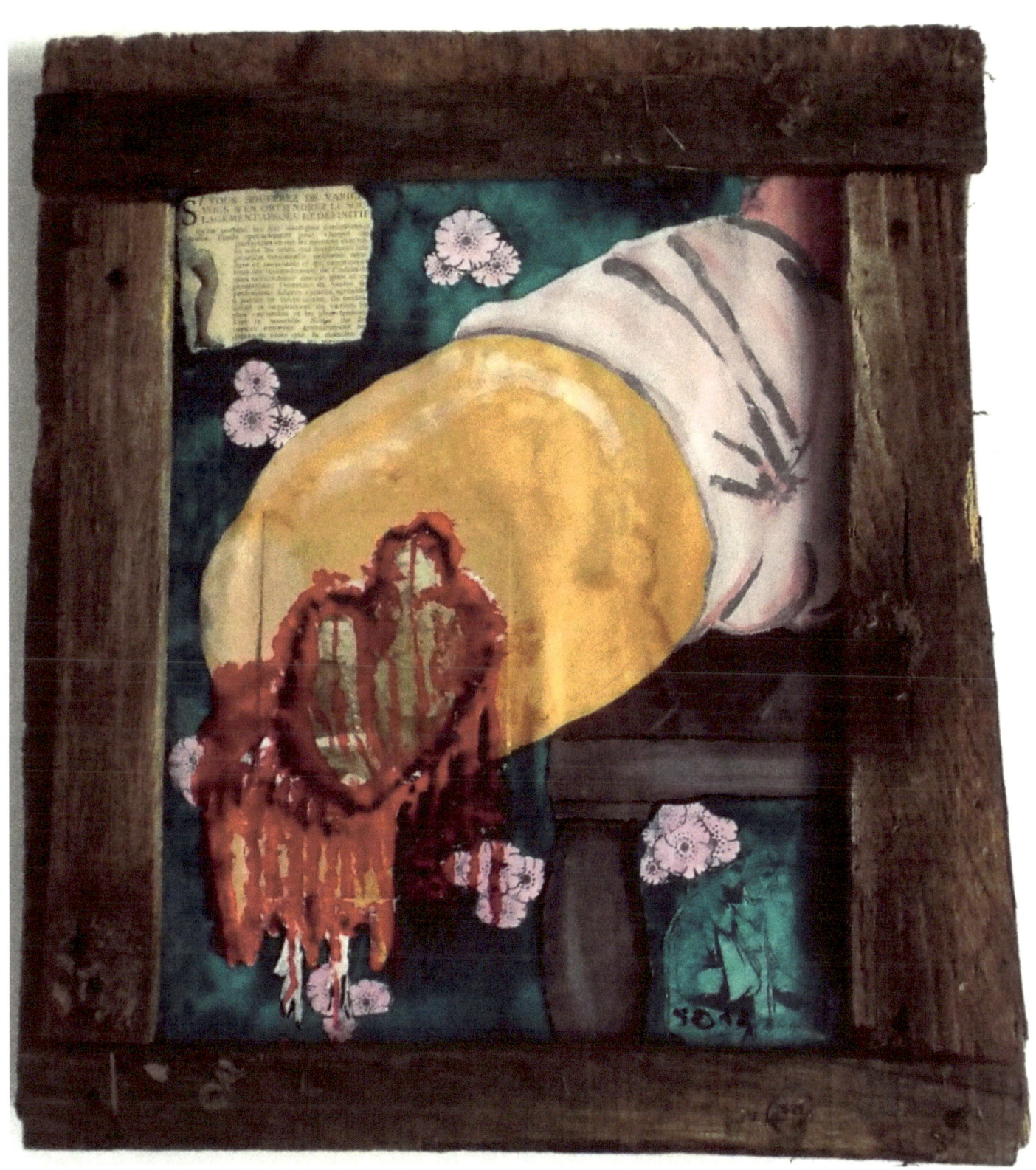

5. A Working Chair Leg.

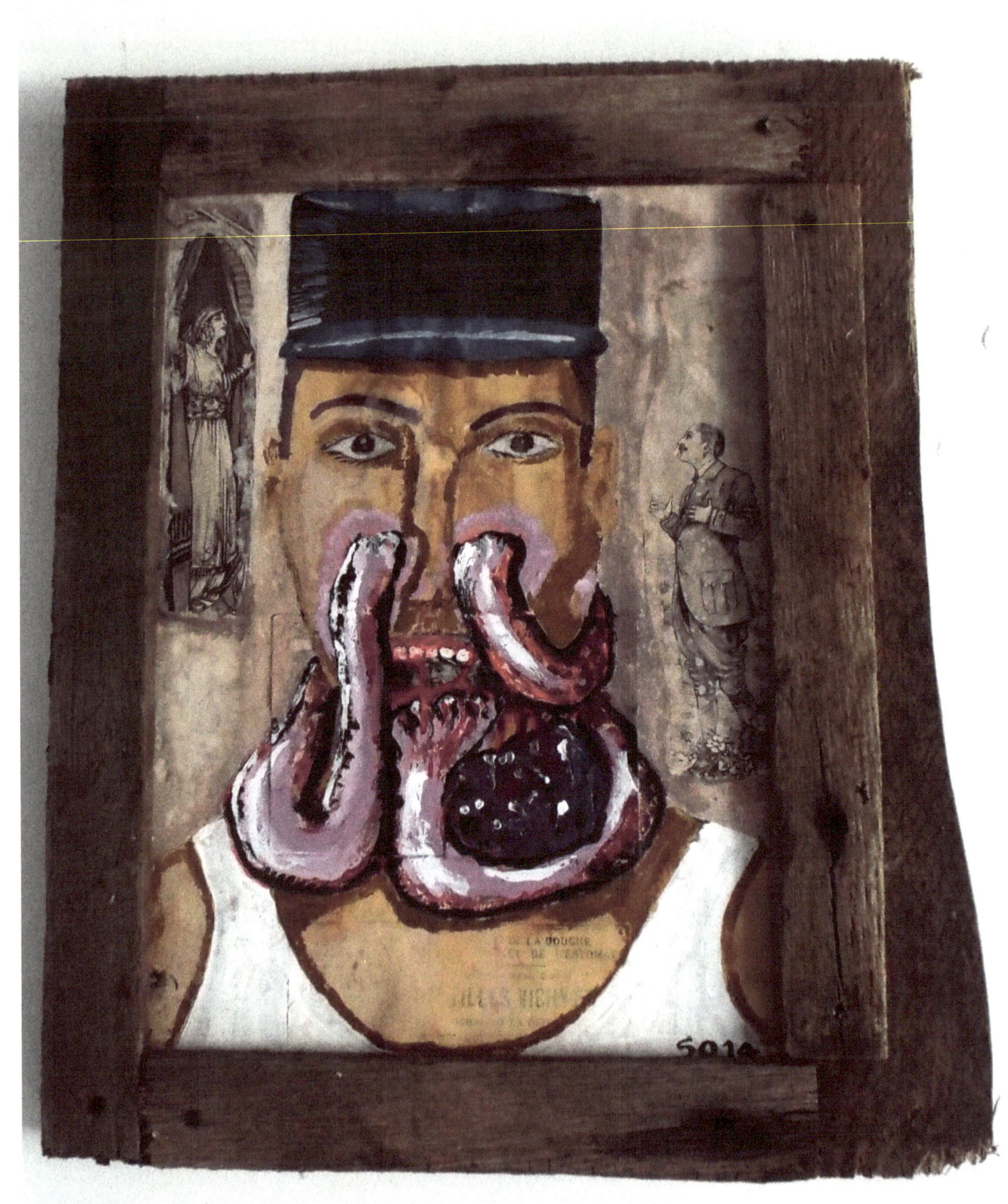

6. The Frustrations Of The Gourmand.

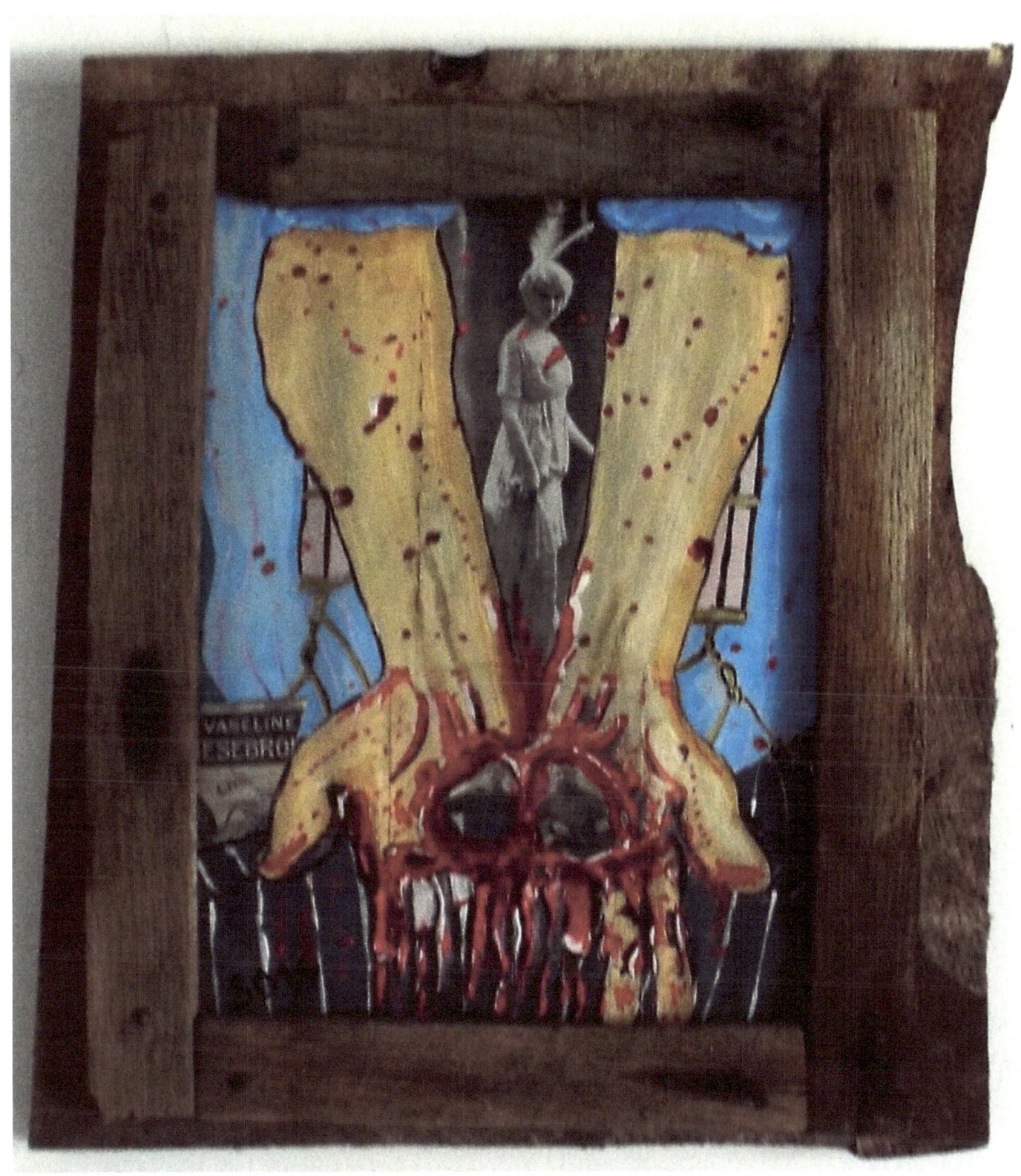

7. The Hands That Caressed.

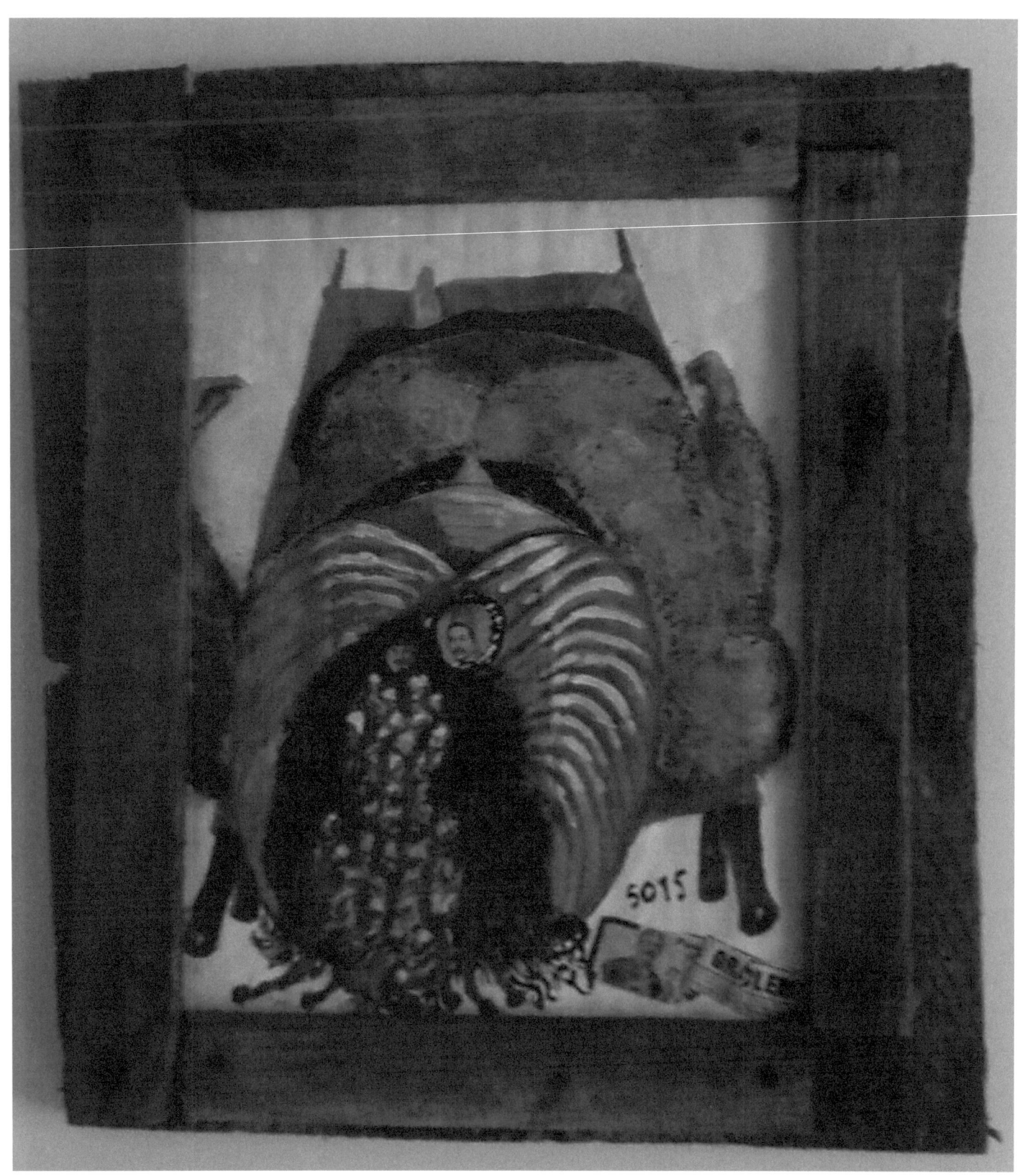

8. Falling.

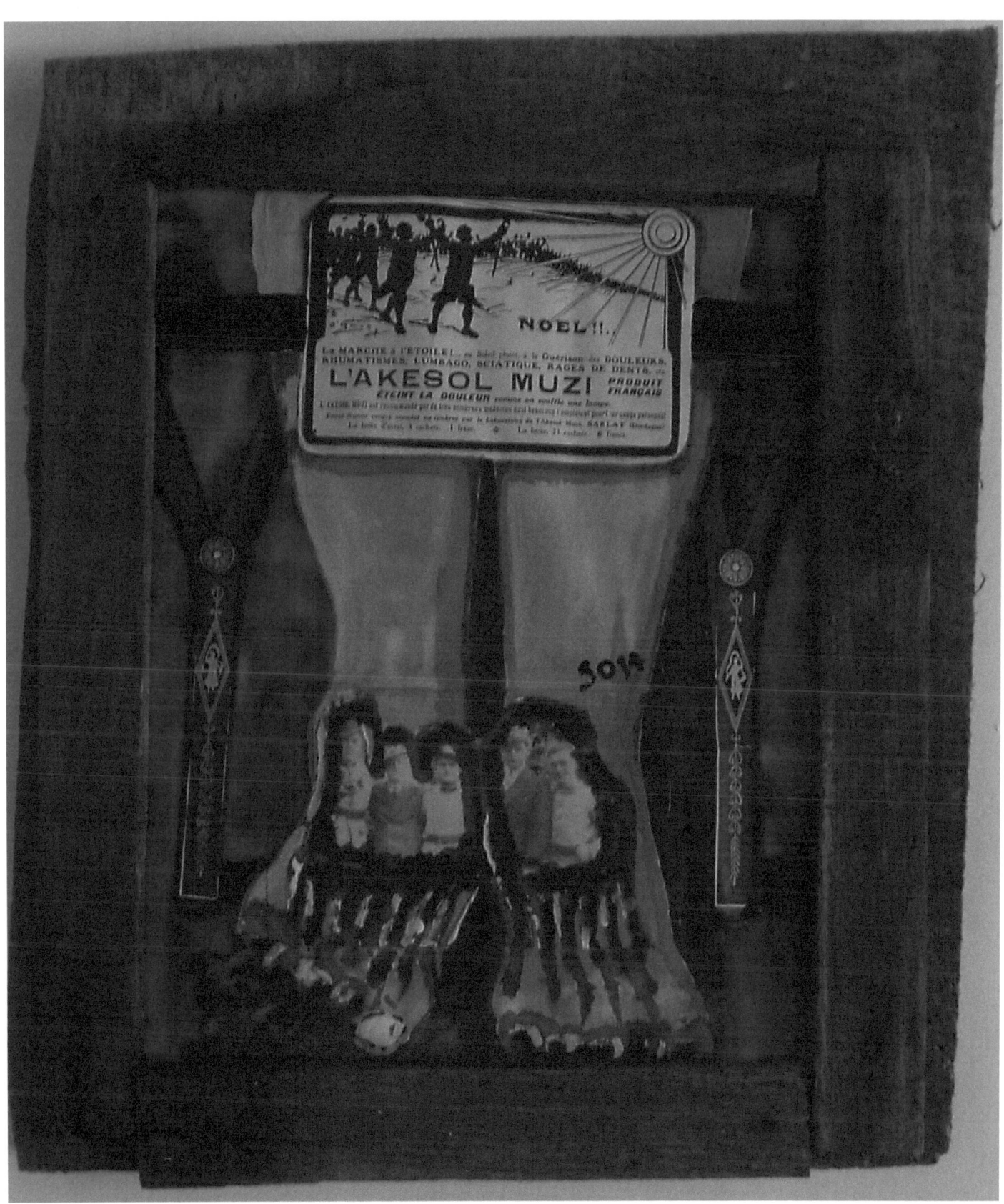

9. Grounding Props.

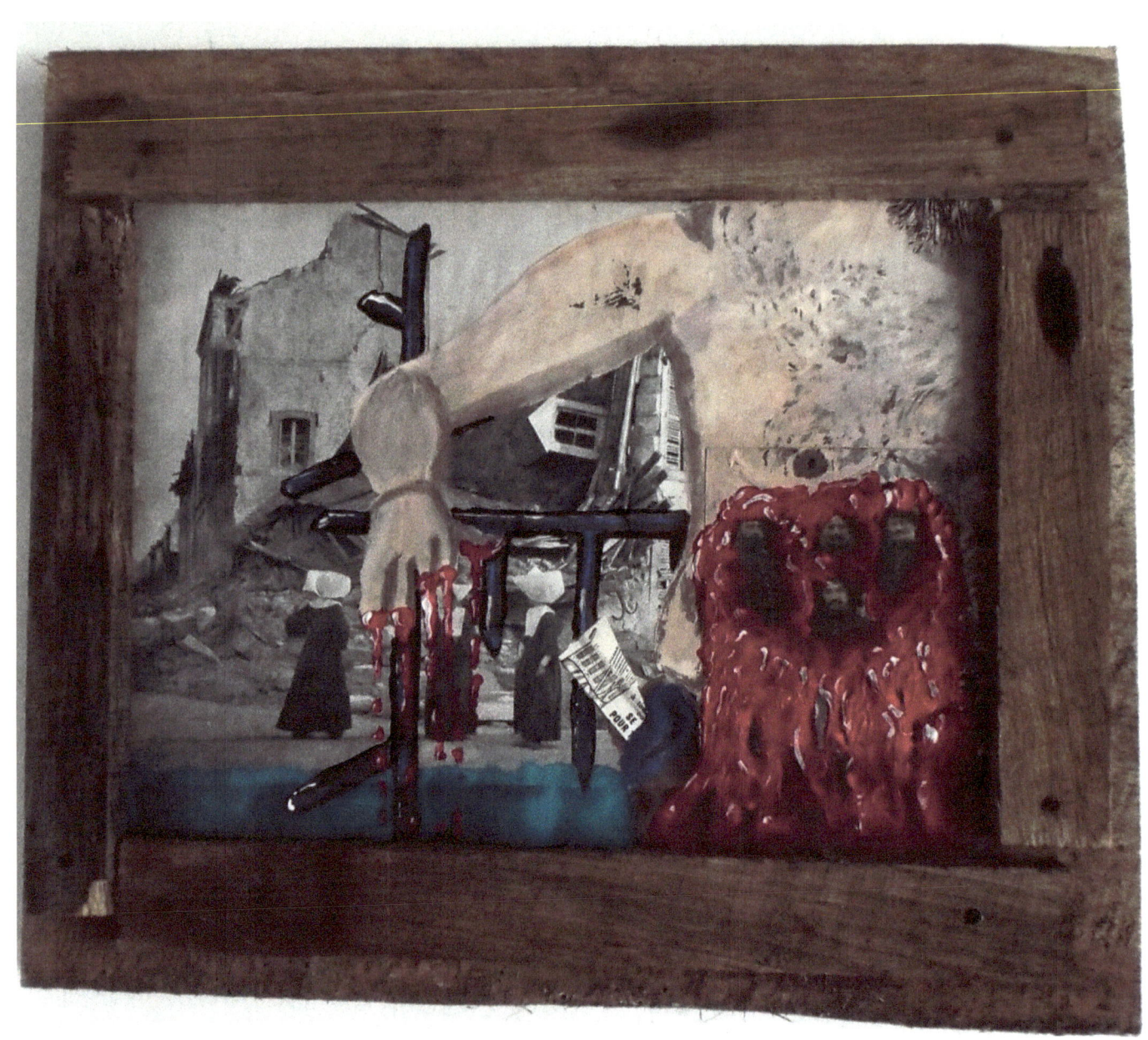

10. Ruined Bodies.

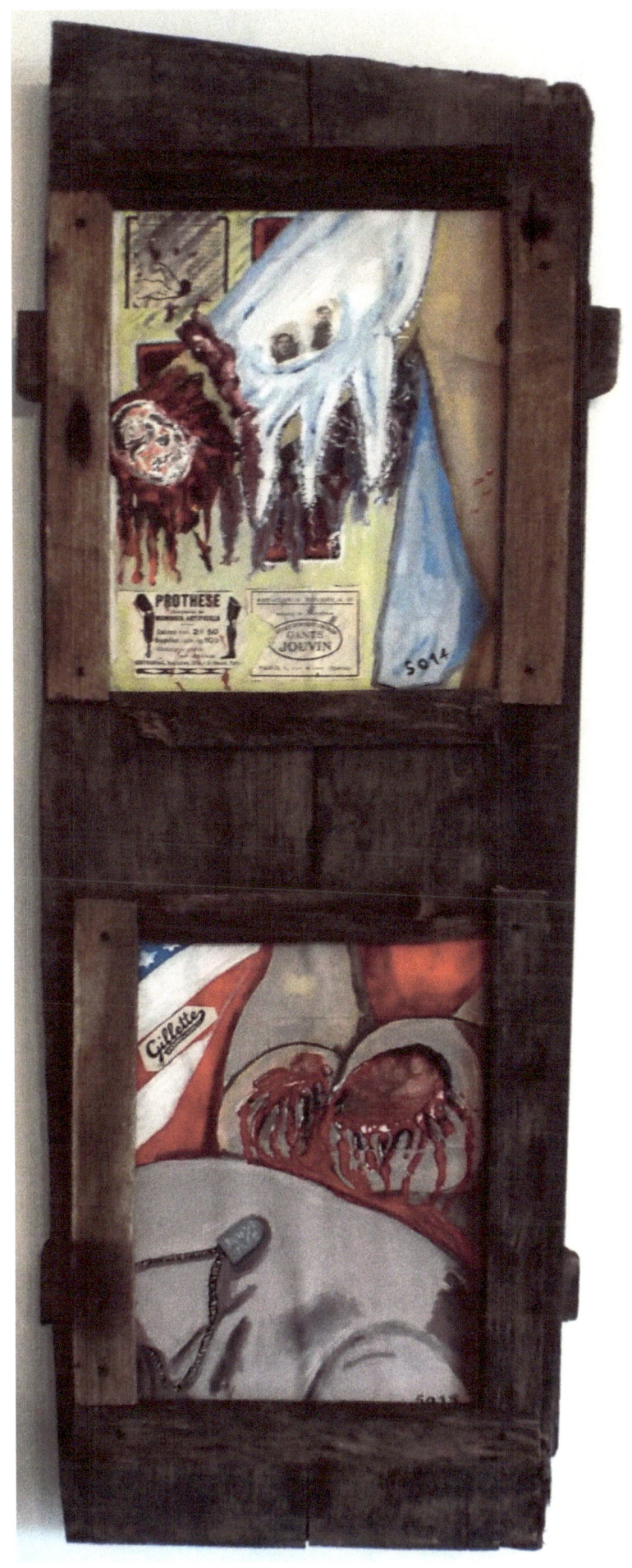

11. Elbowed Out. (Top)

12. Badass Enemy.

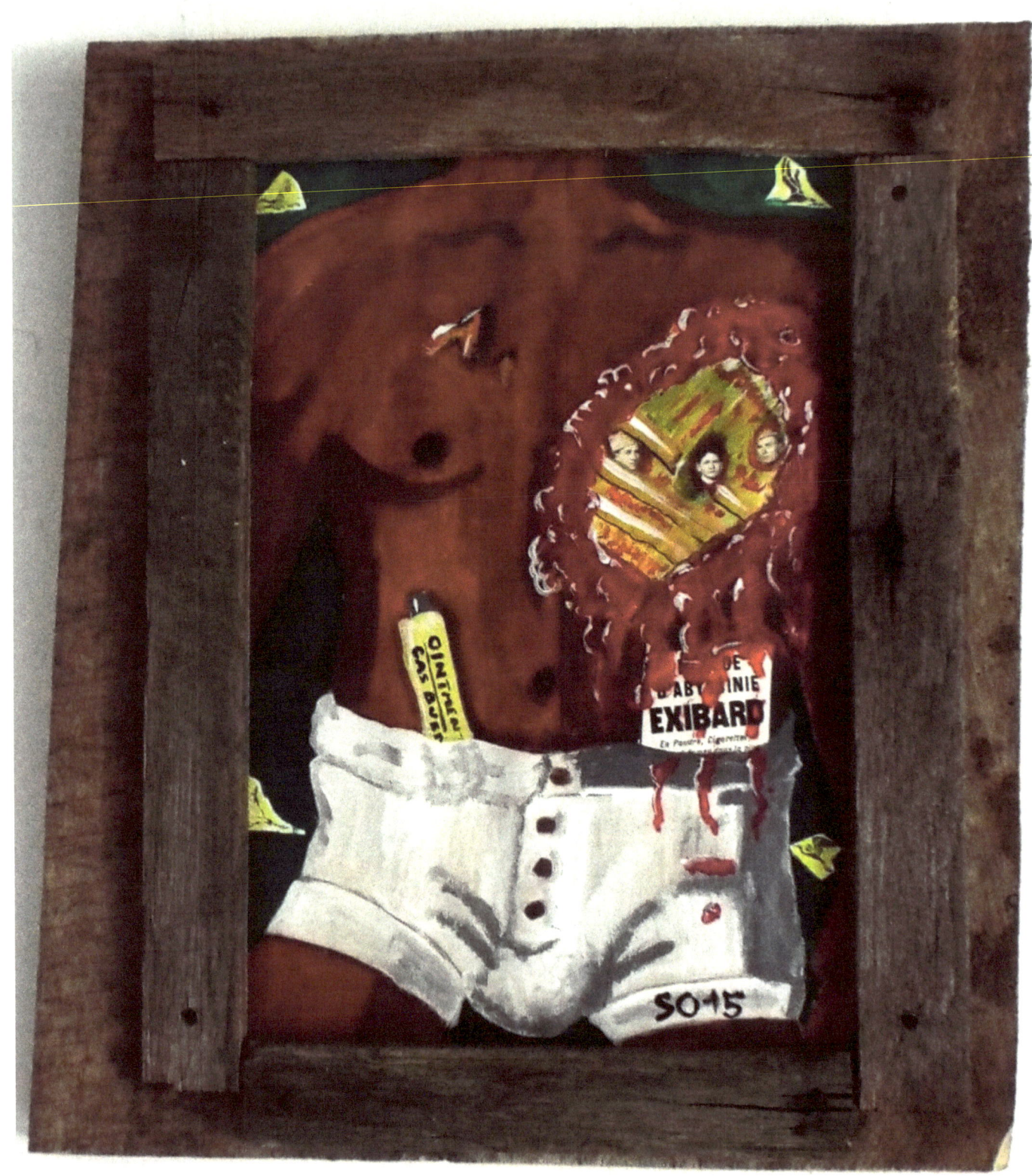

13. Blind Side.

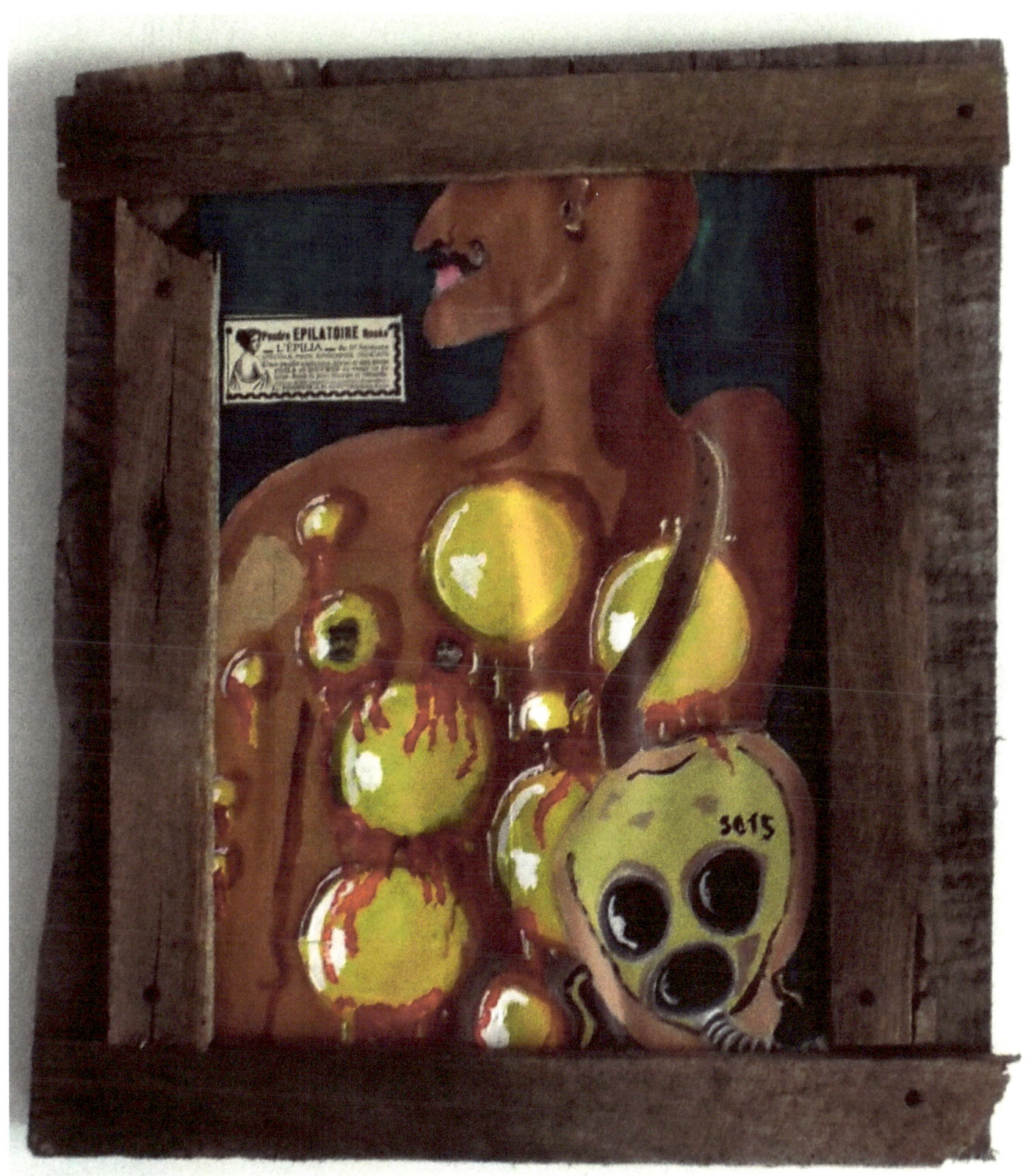

14. Exuding.

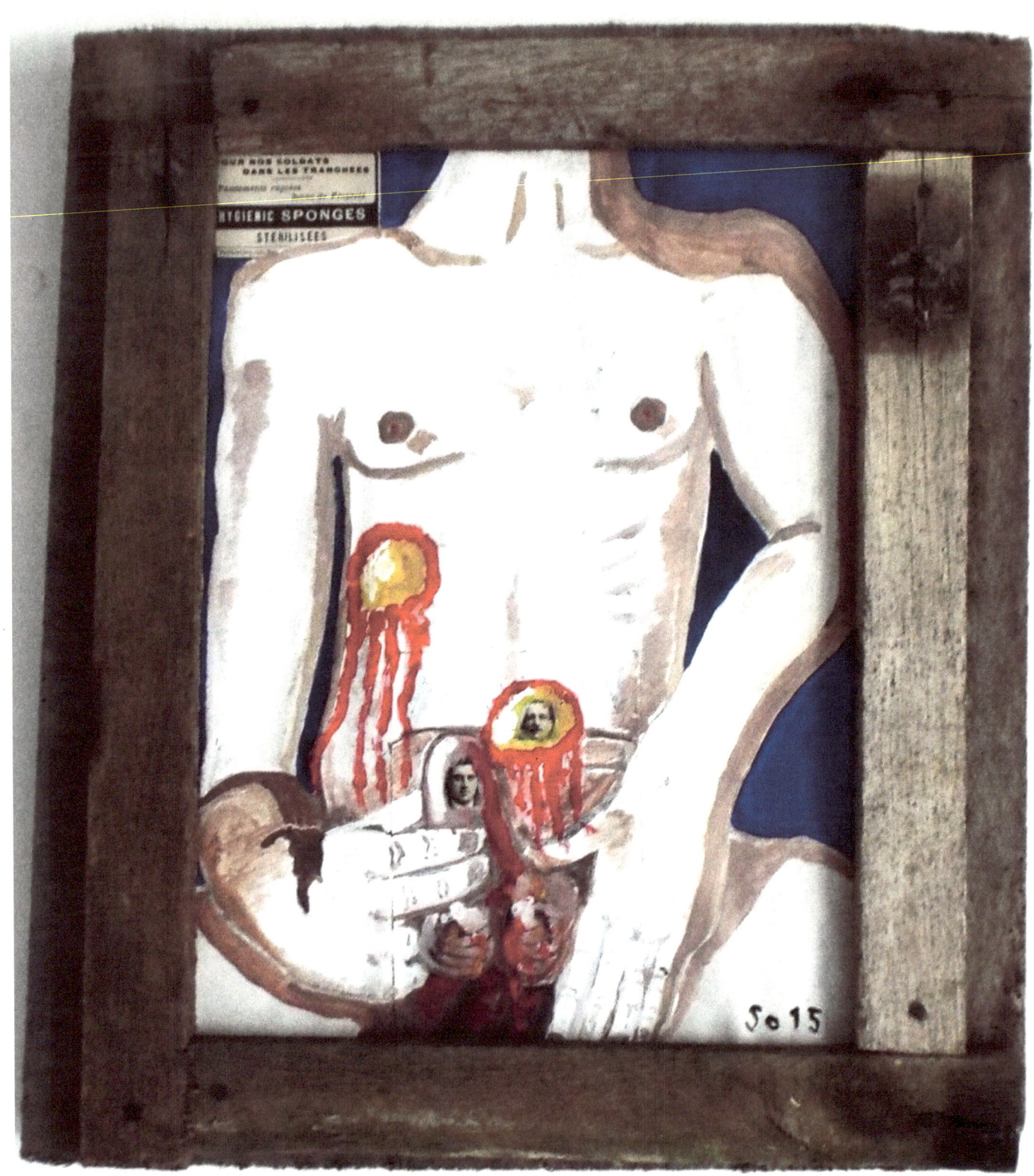

15. Decimated Manhood.

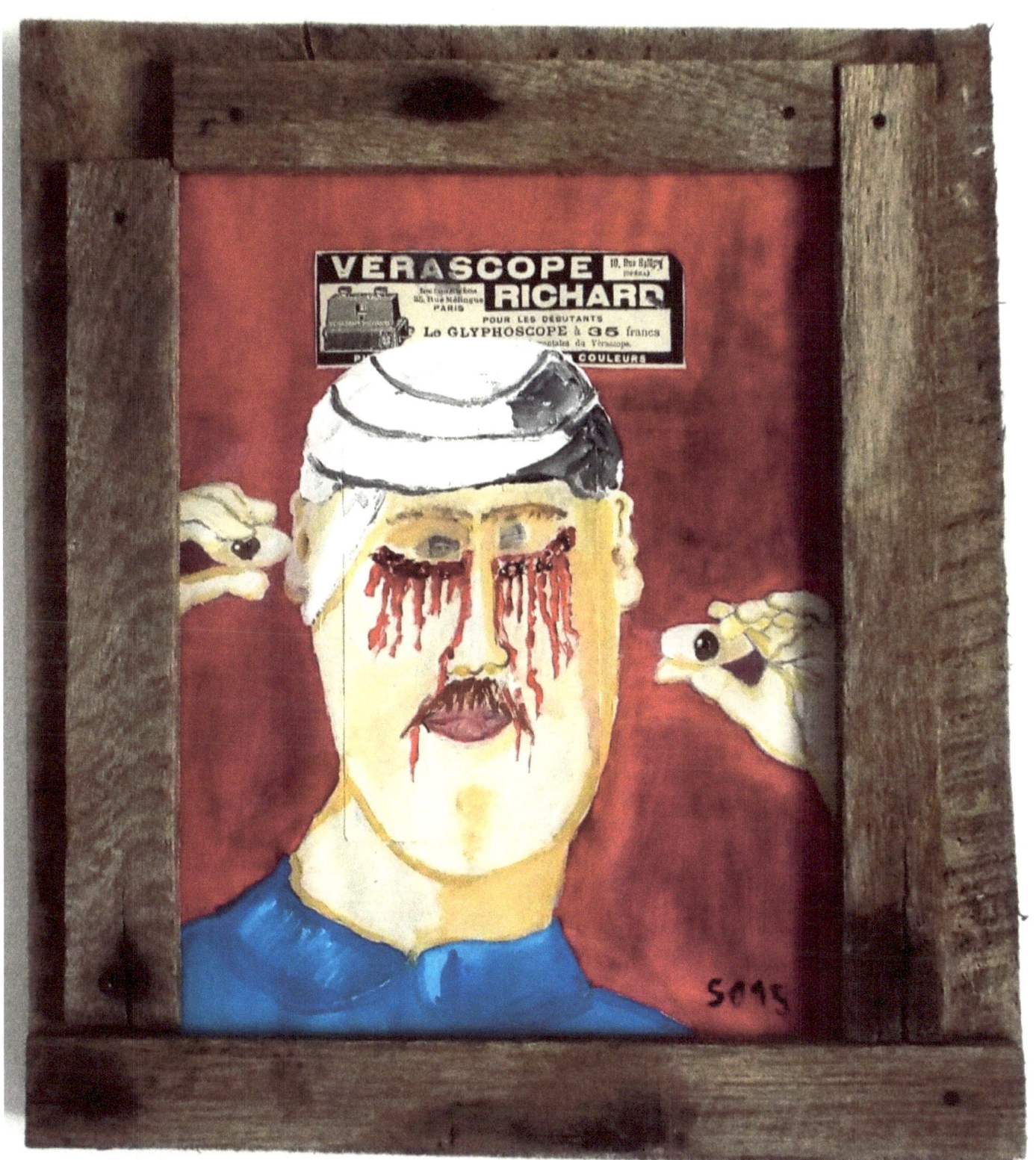

16. The Eyes Have It.

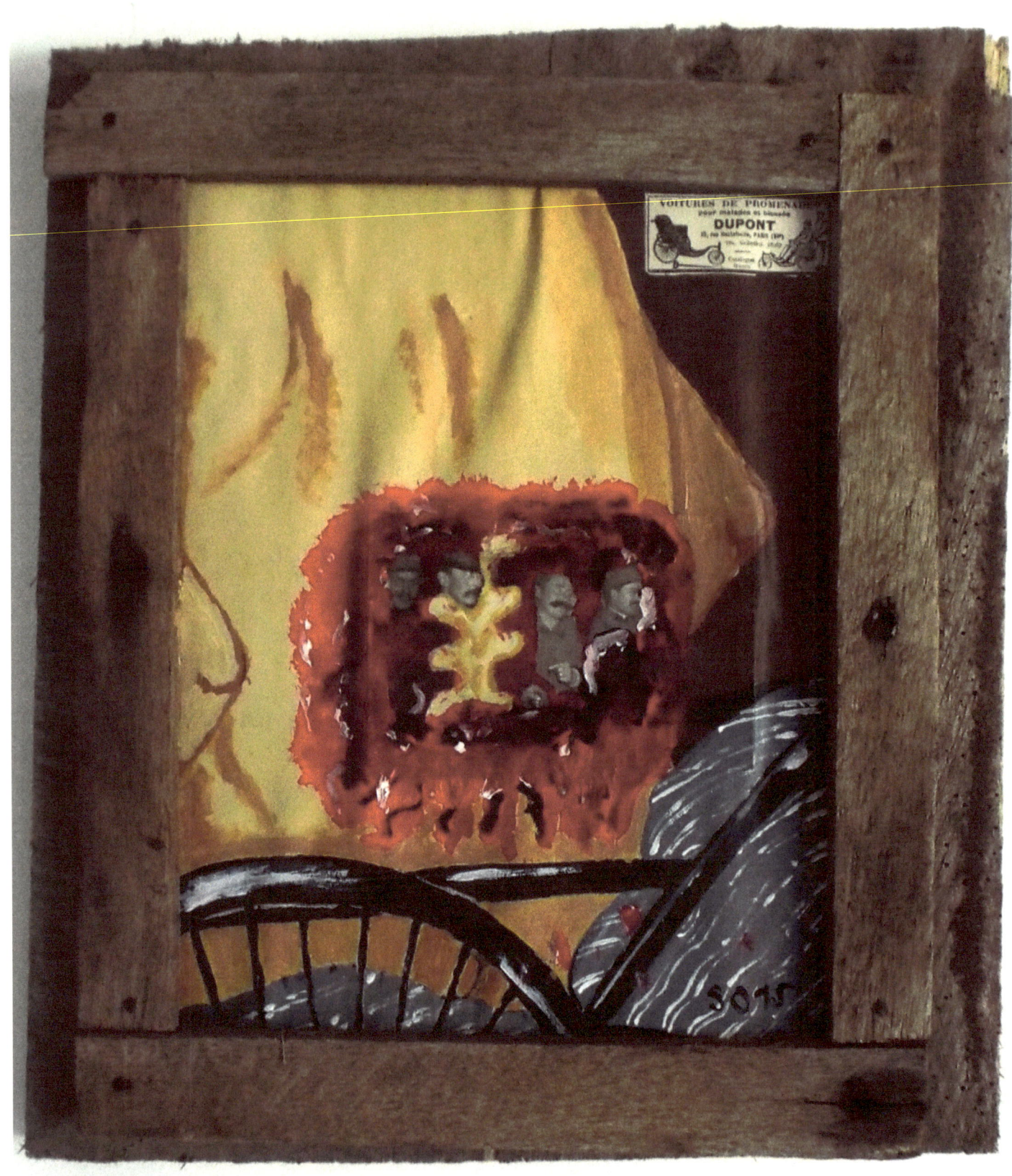

17. Sit Down, No Fuss.

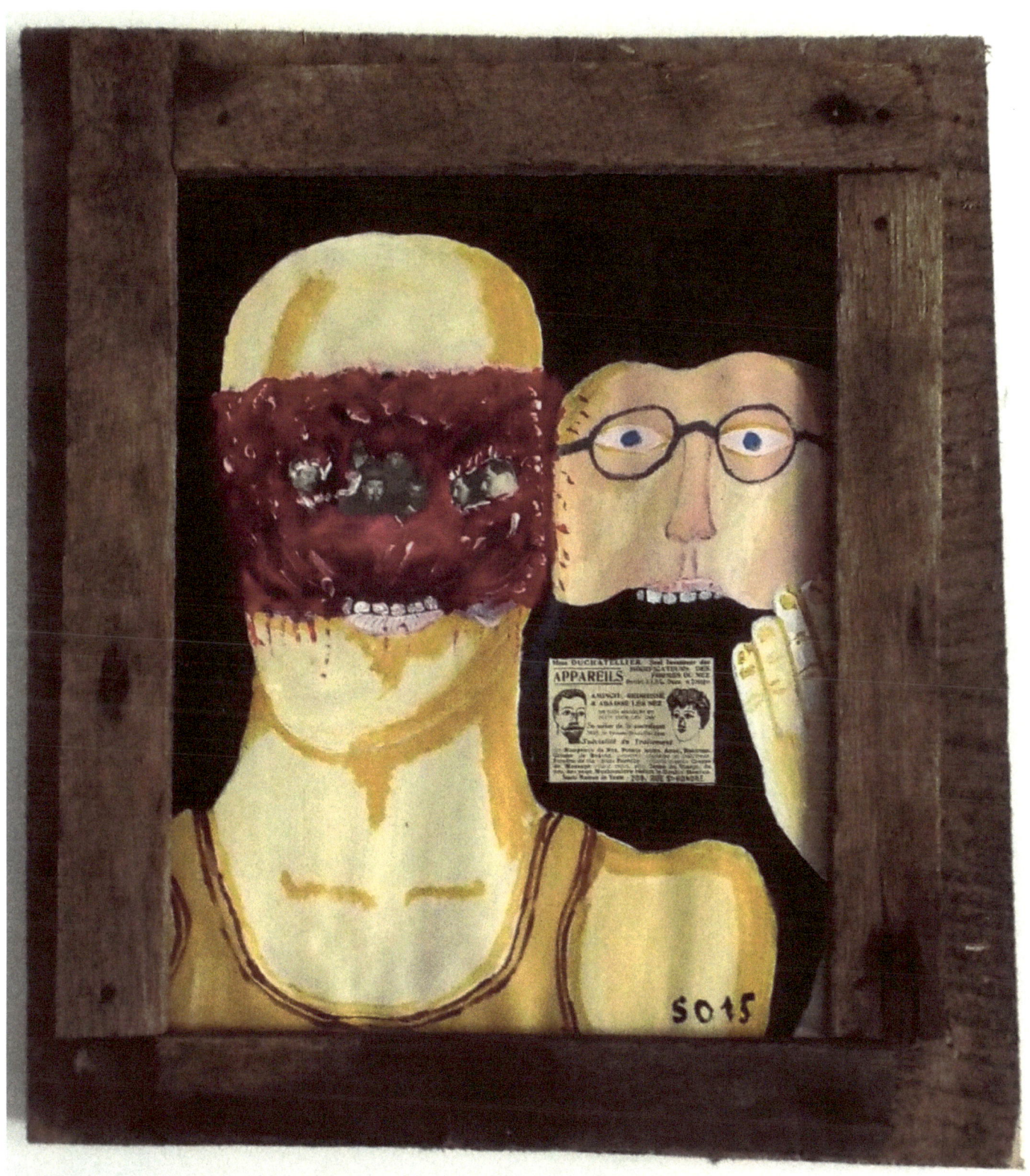

18. Face Off, Face On.

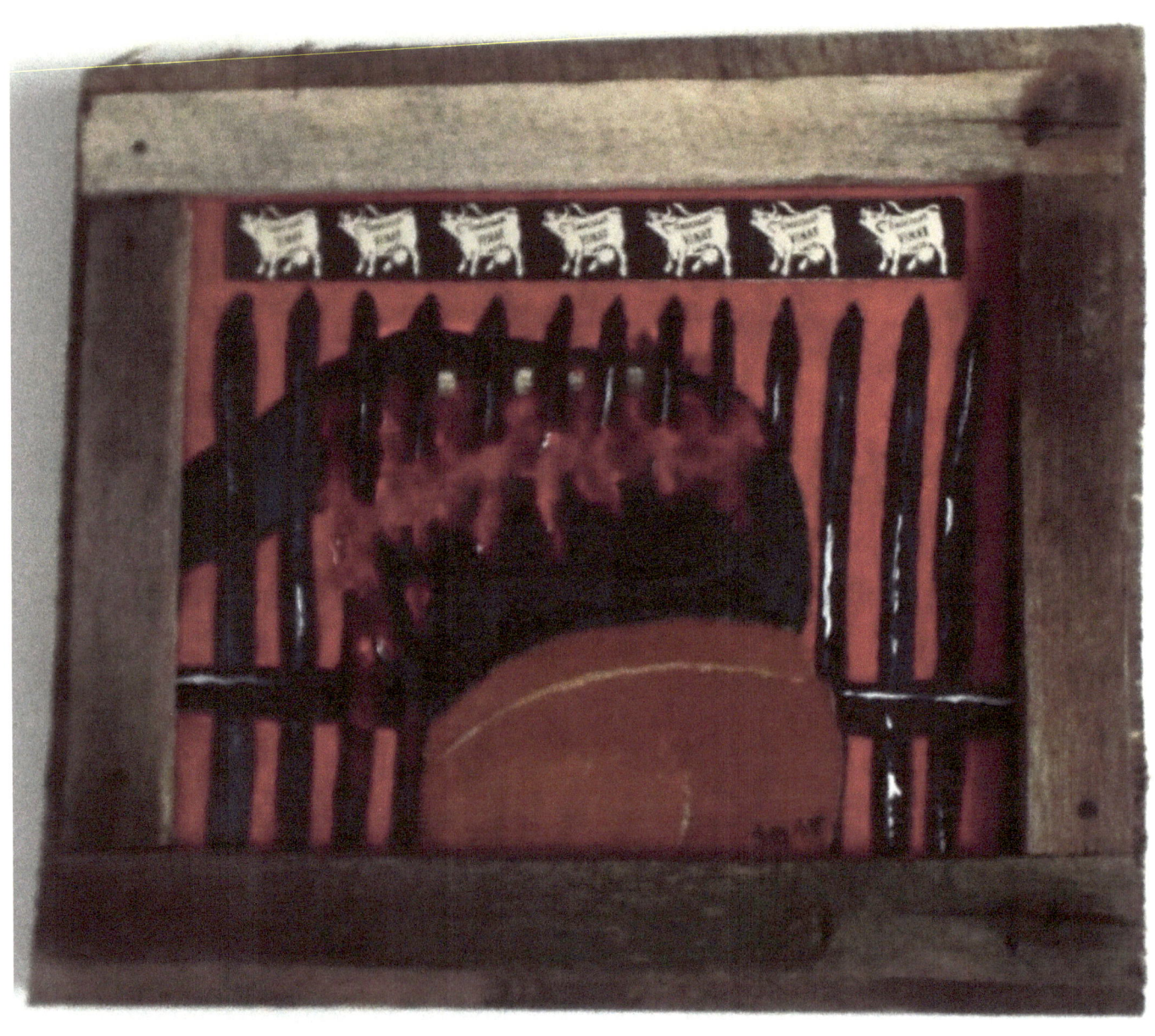

19. What Is The Point?

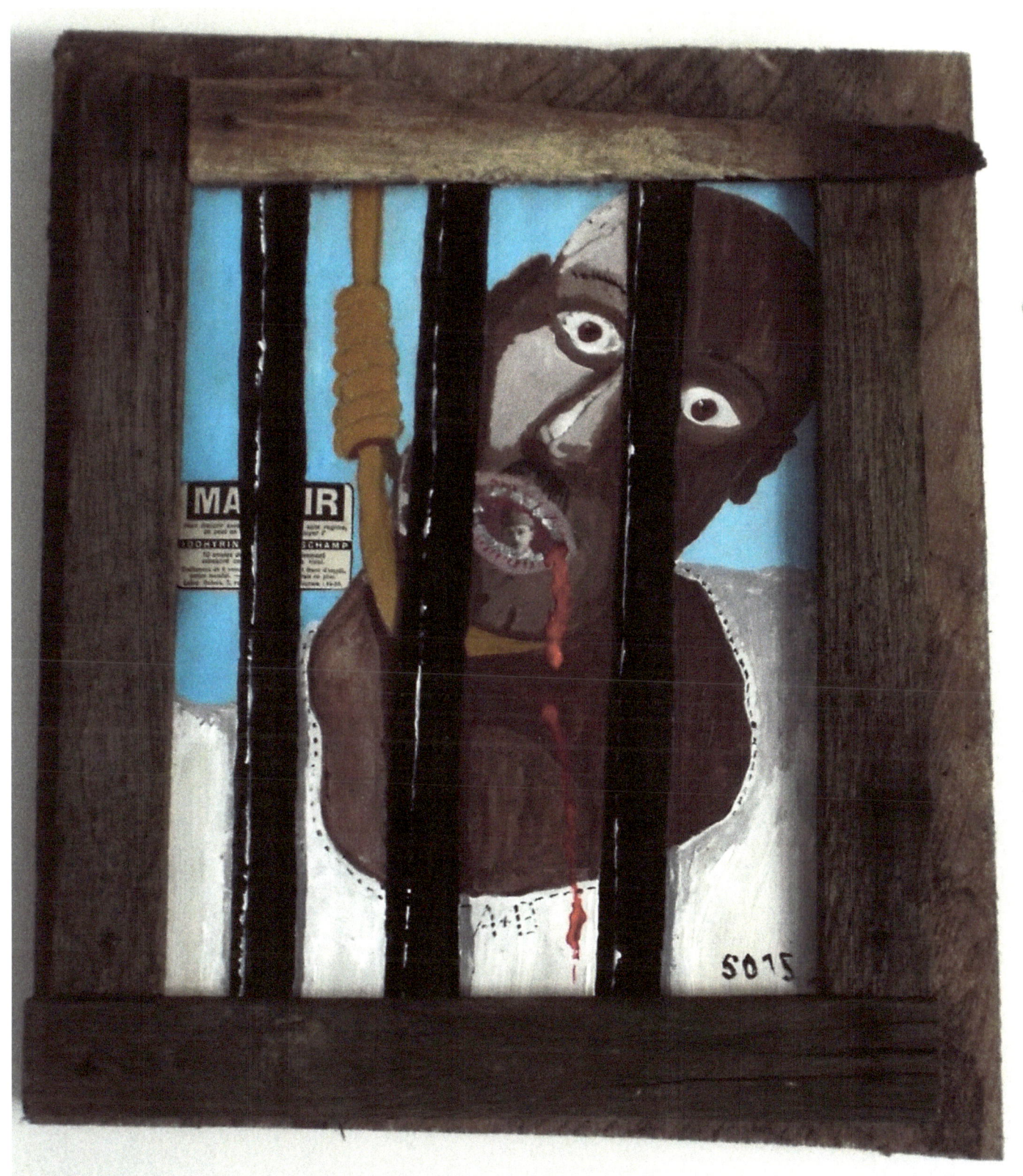

20. No Choice Hero.

THE PROCESS.

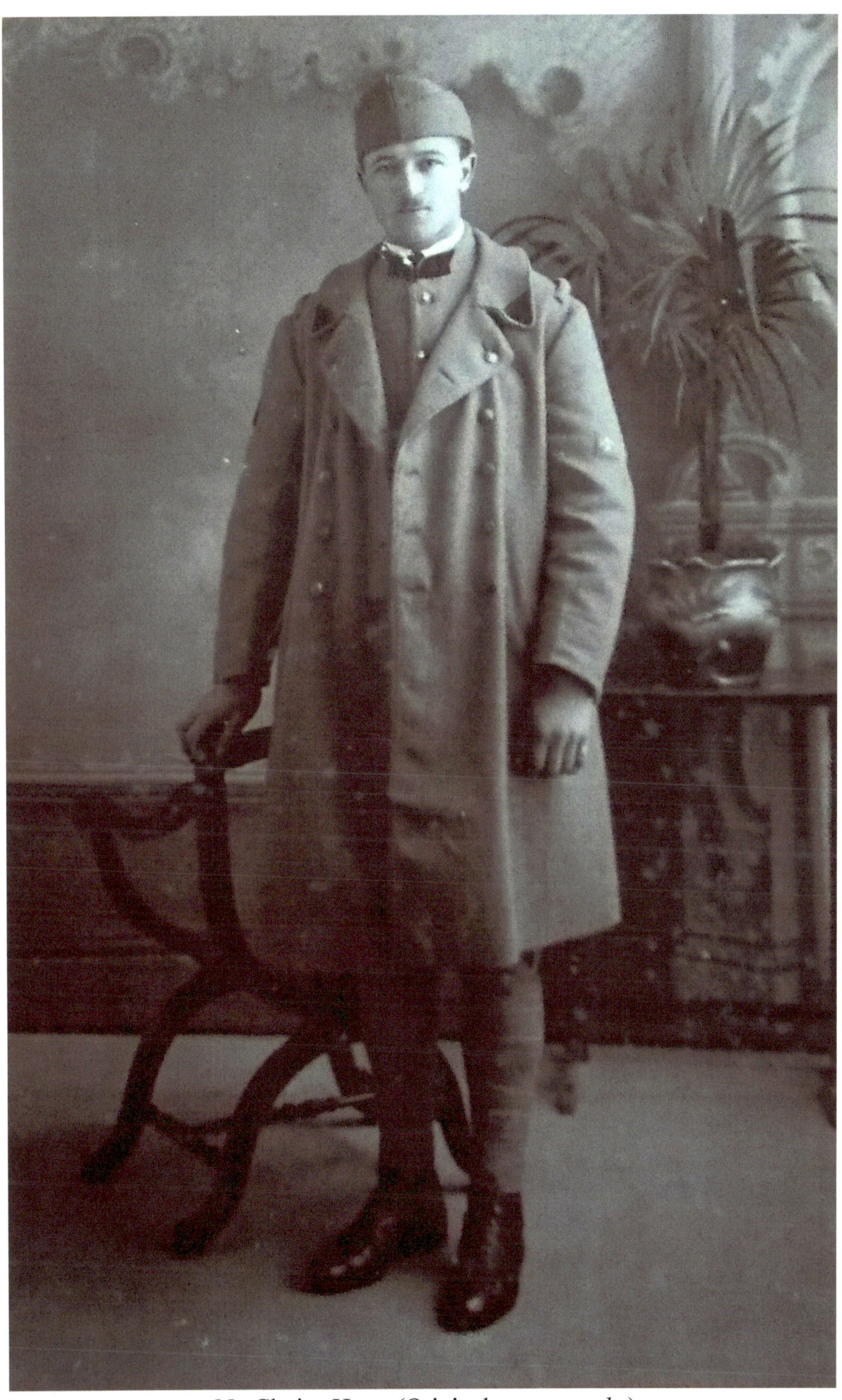

No Choice Hero. (Original *carte postale*.)

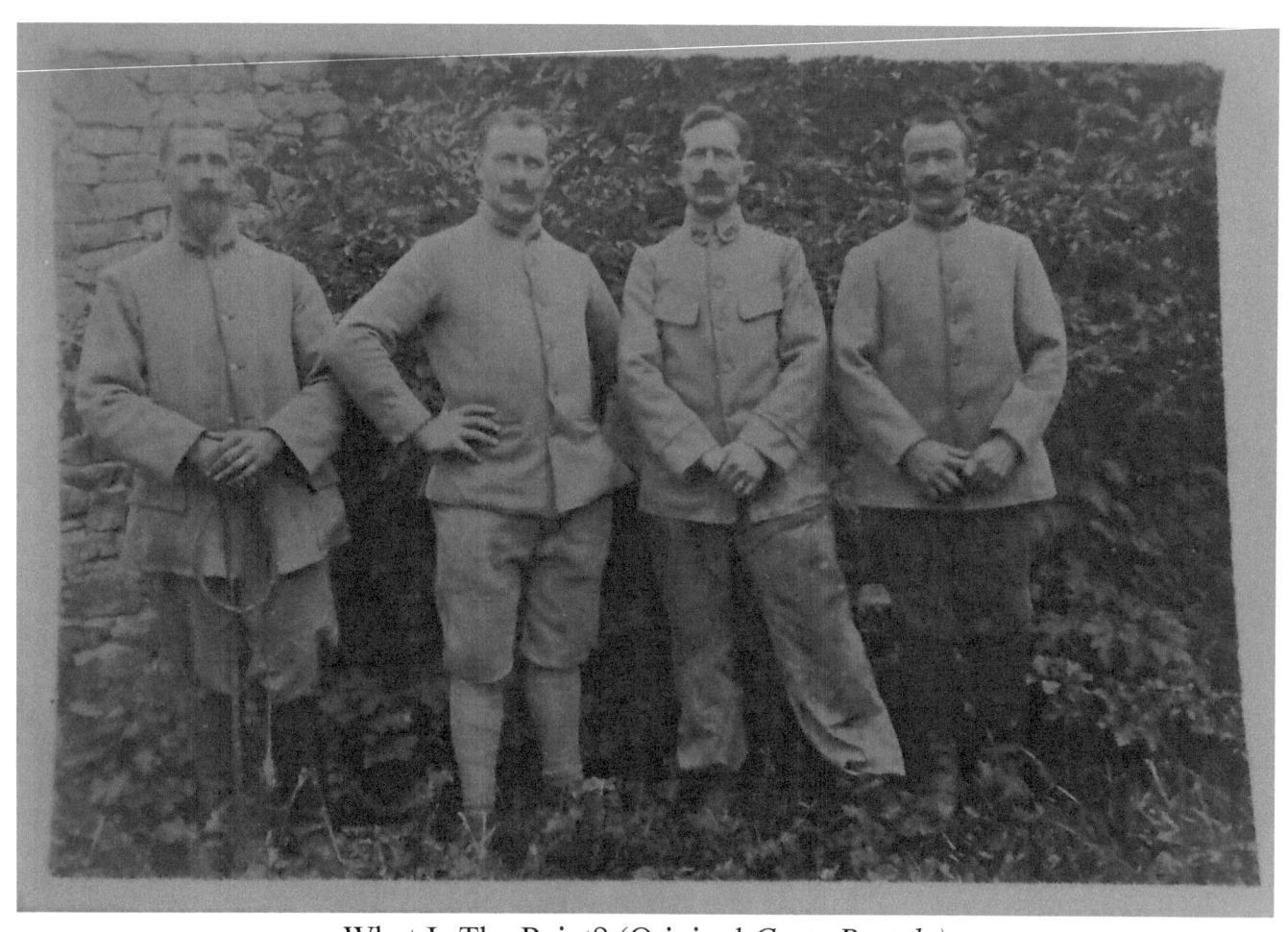

What Is The Point? (Original *Carte Postale)*

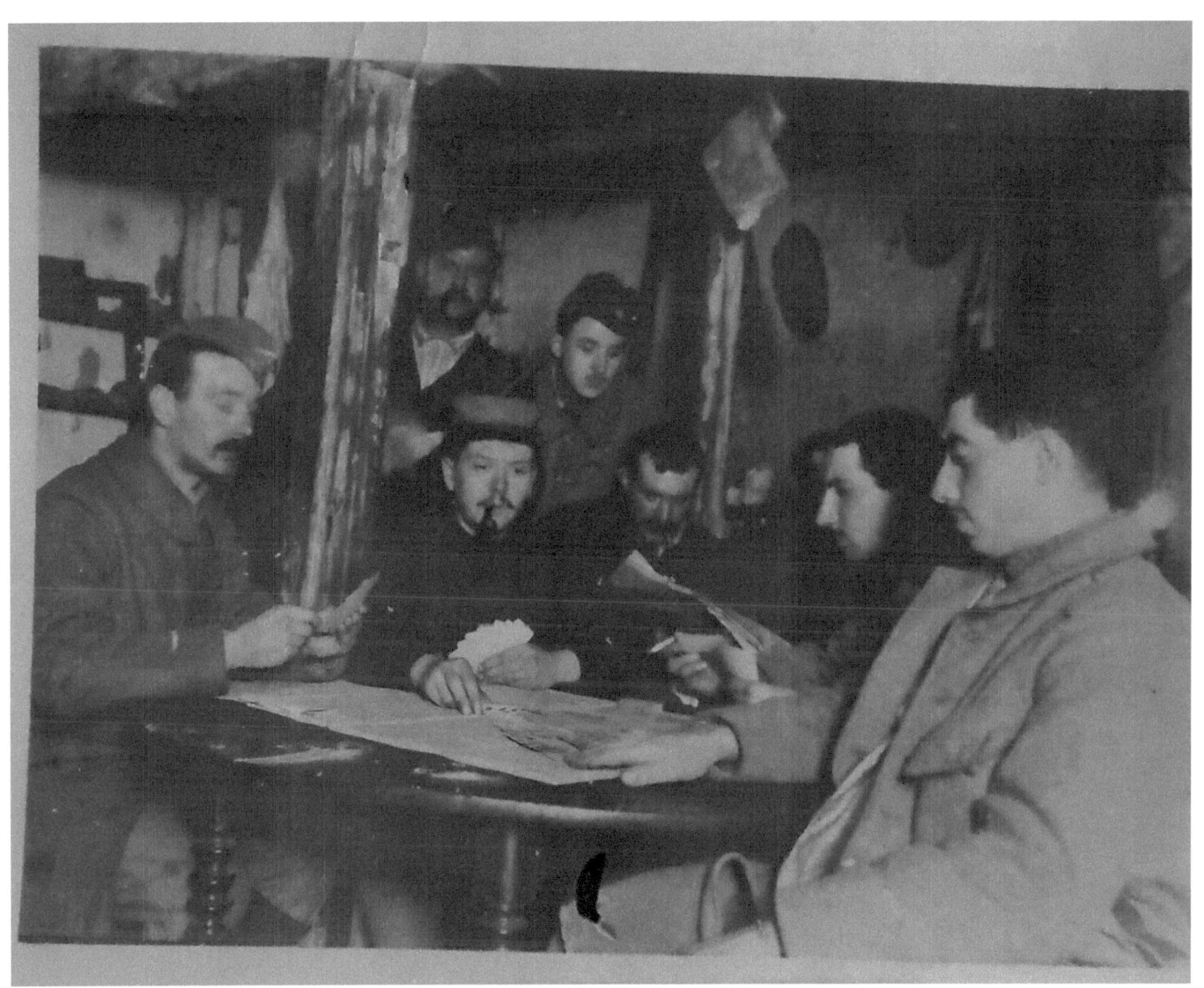

Face Off, Face On. (Original *carte postale)*

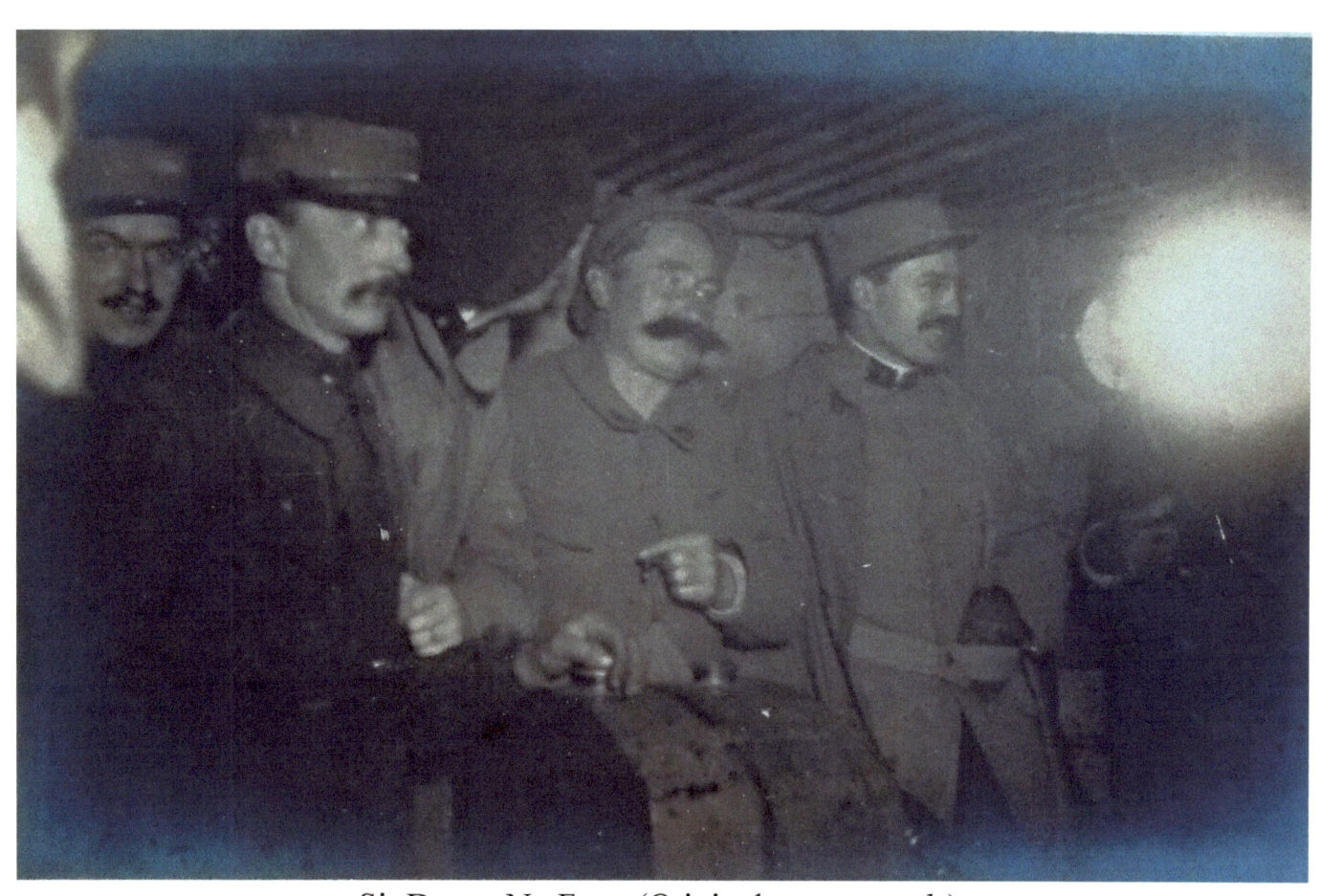

Sit Down, No Fuss. (Original *carte postale*).

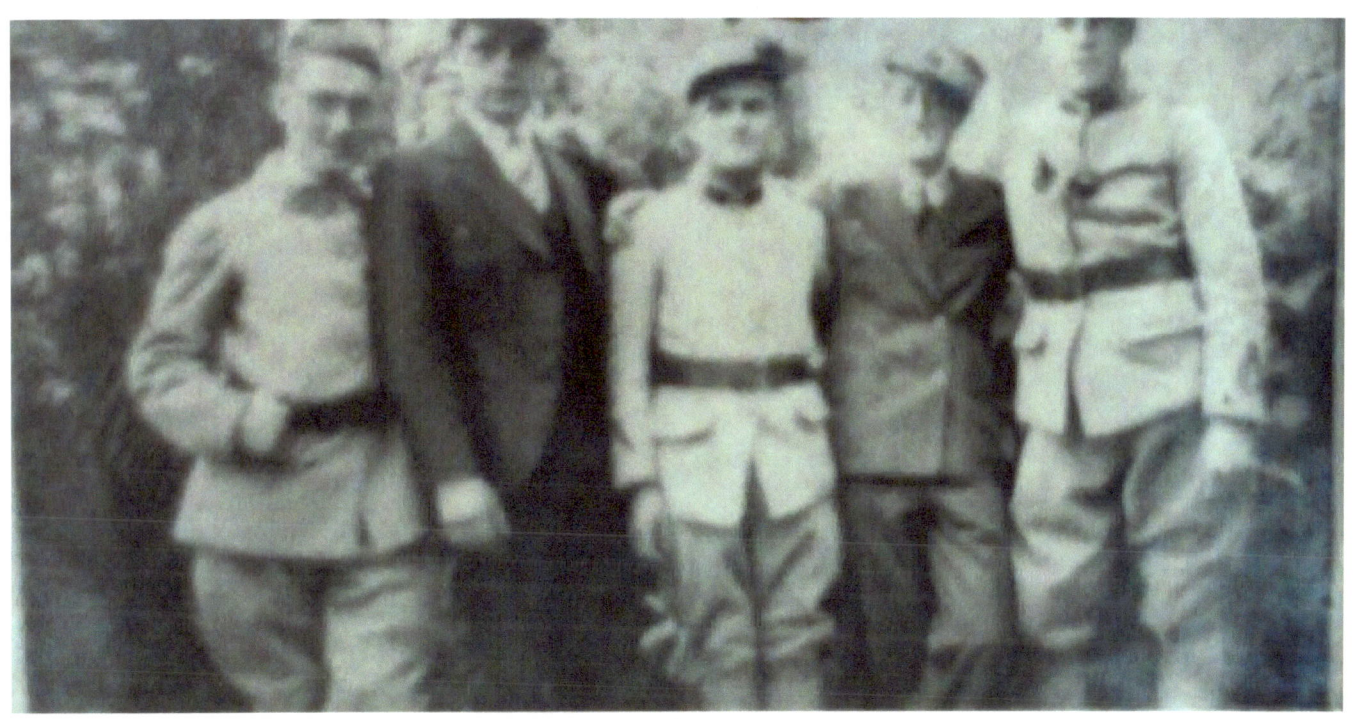

Grounding Props. (Original *carte postale)*.

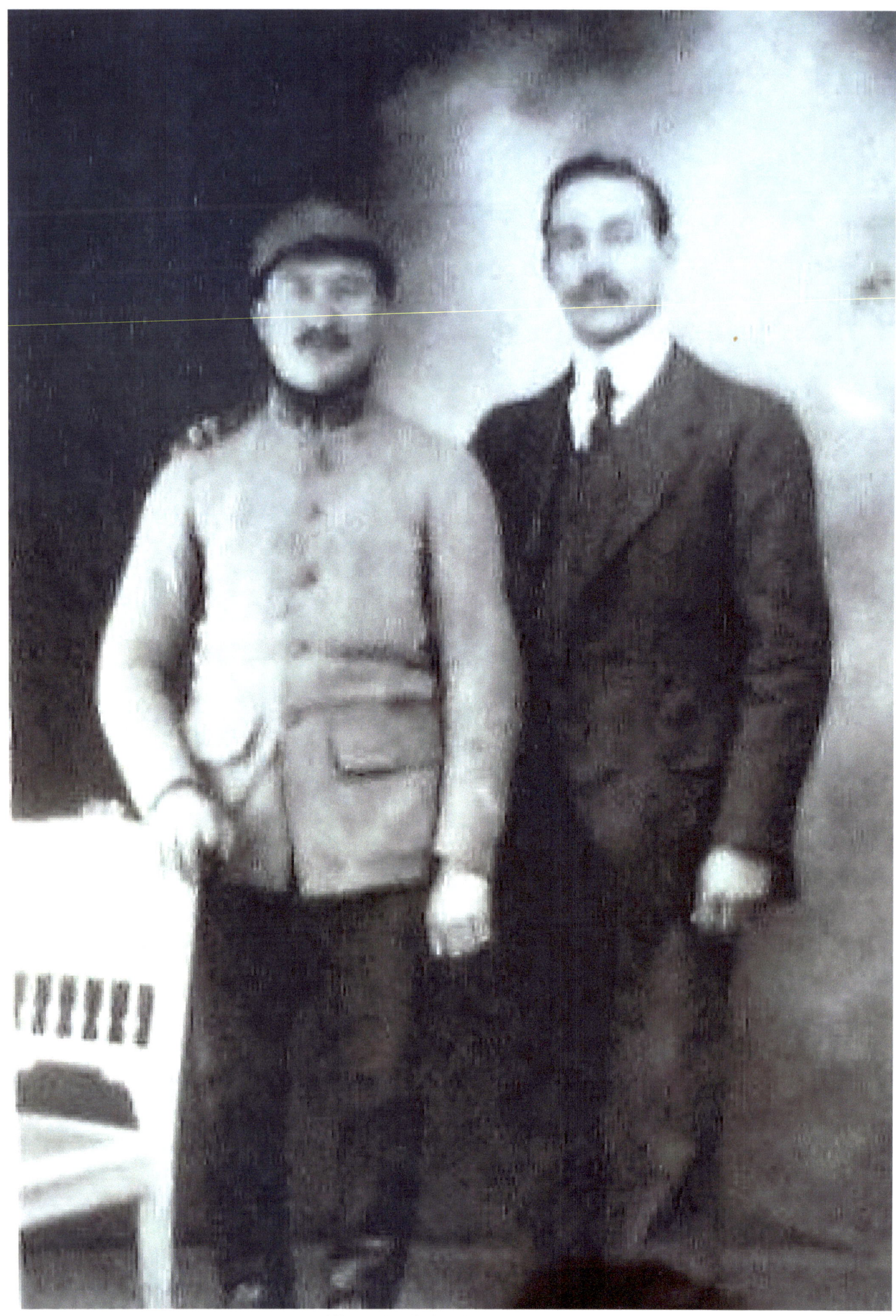

Falling. (Original *carte postale*).

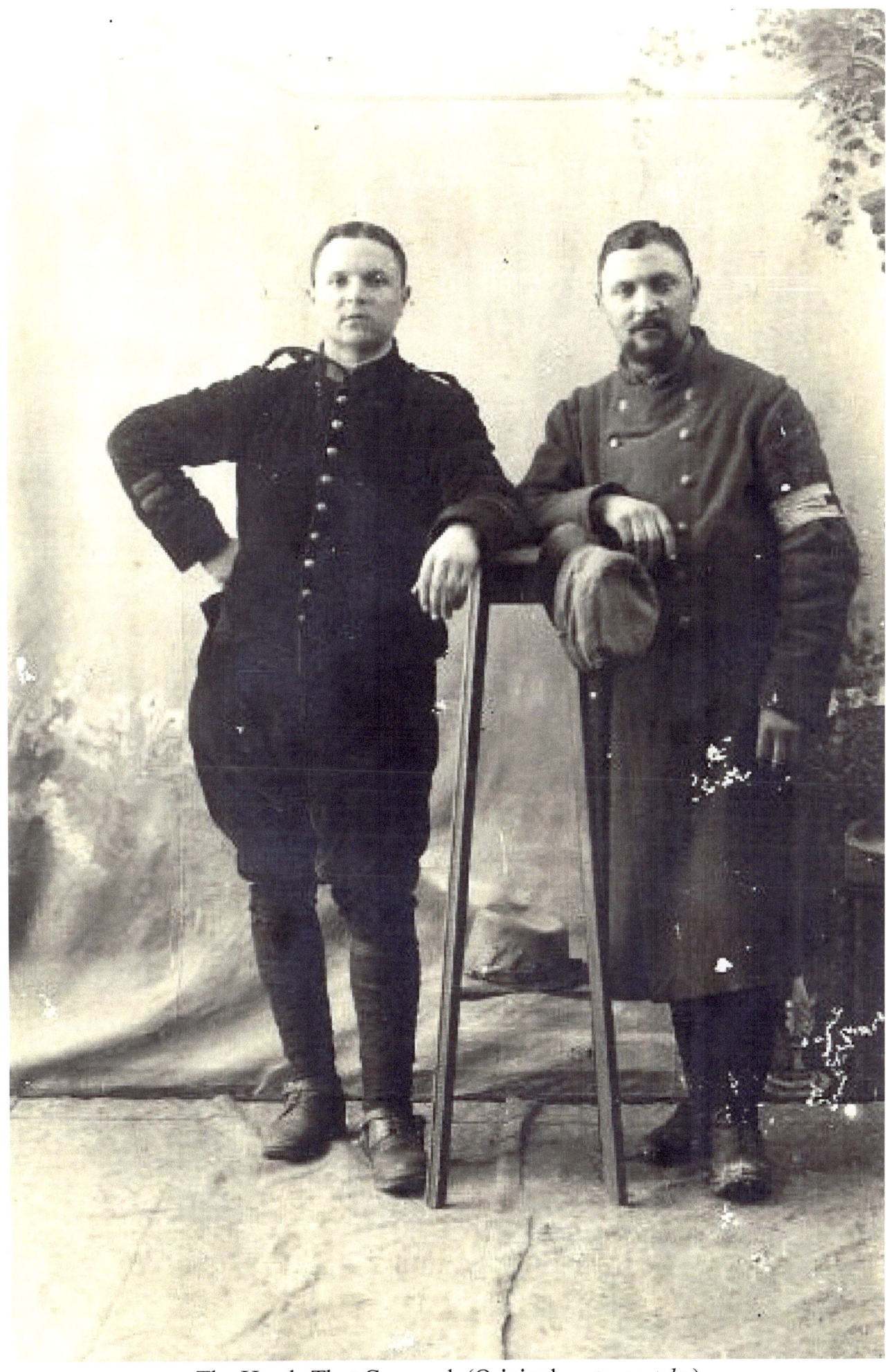

The Hands That Caressed. (Original *carte postale*.)

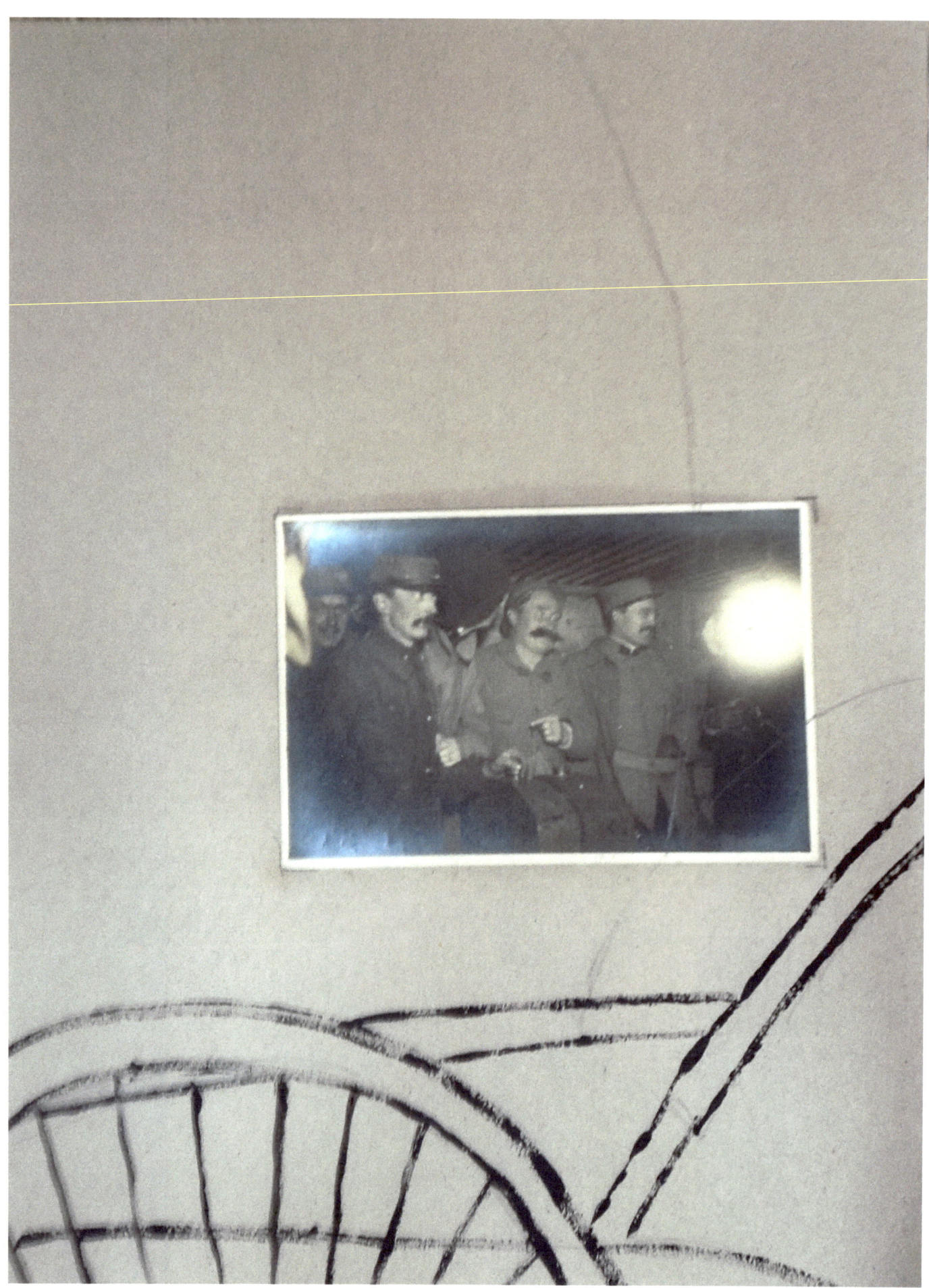

Sit Down, No Fuss.

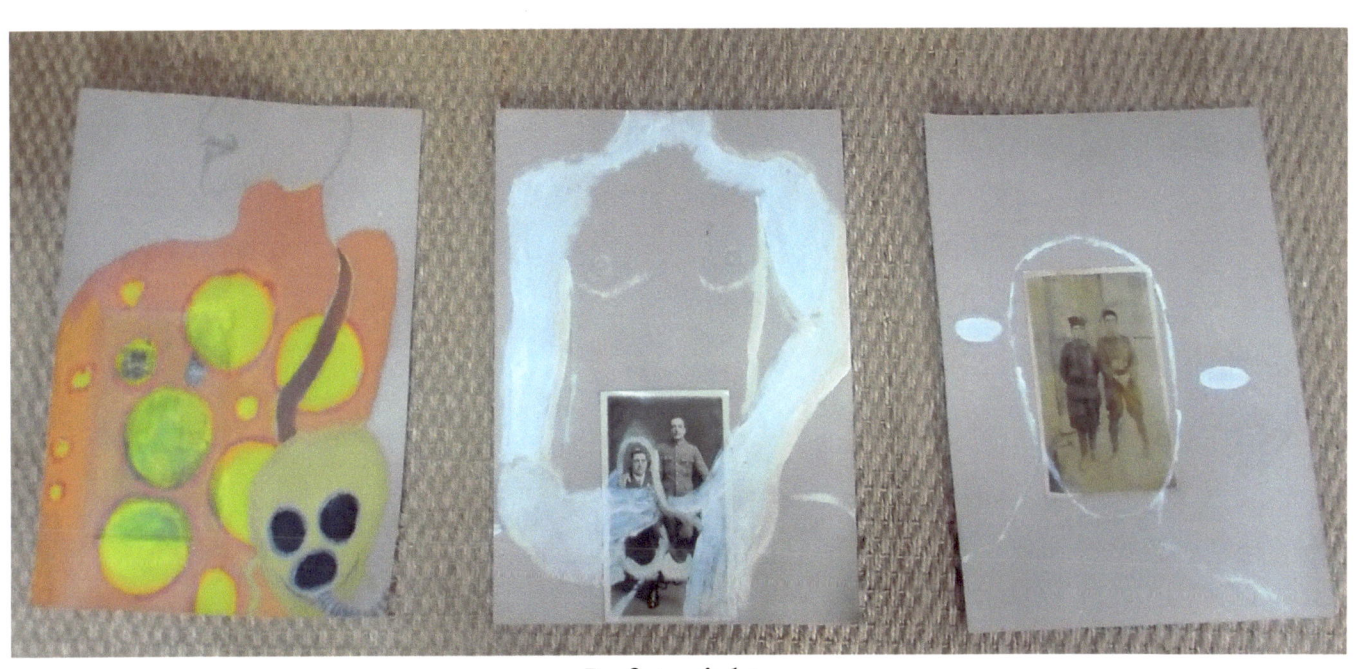

Left to right:

Exuding, Decimated Manhood, The Eyes Have It.

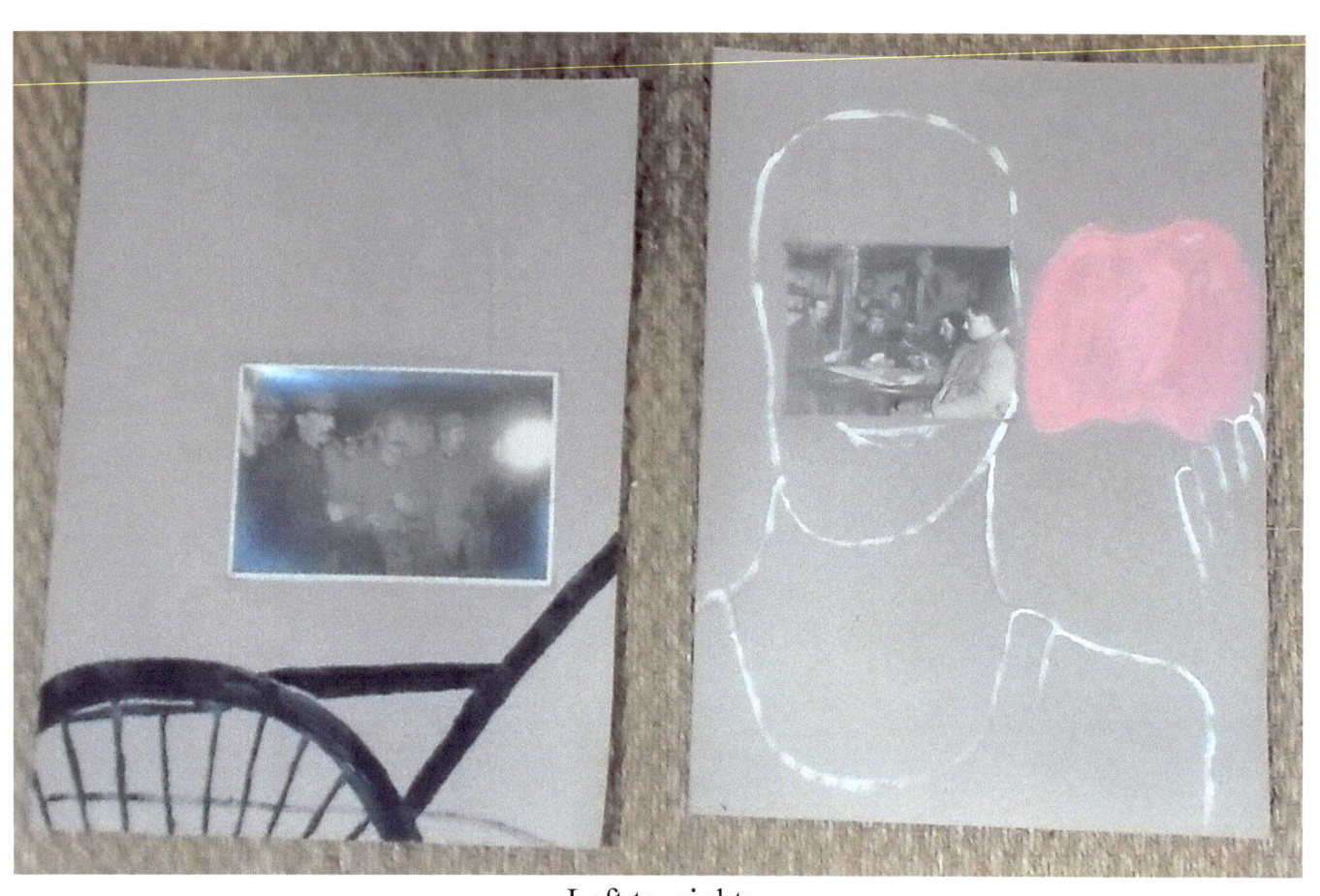

Left to right:

Sit Down, No Fuss; Face off, Face On.

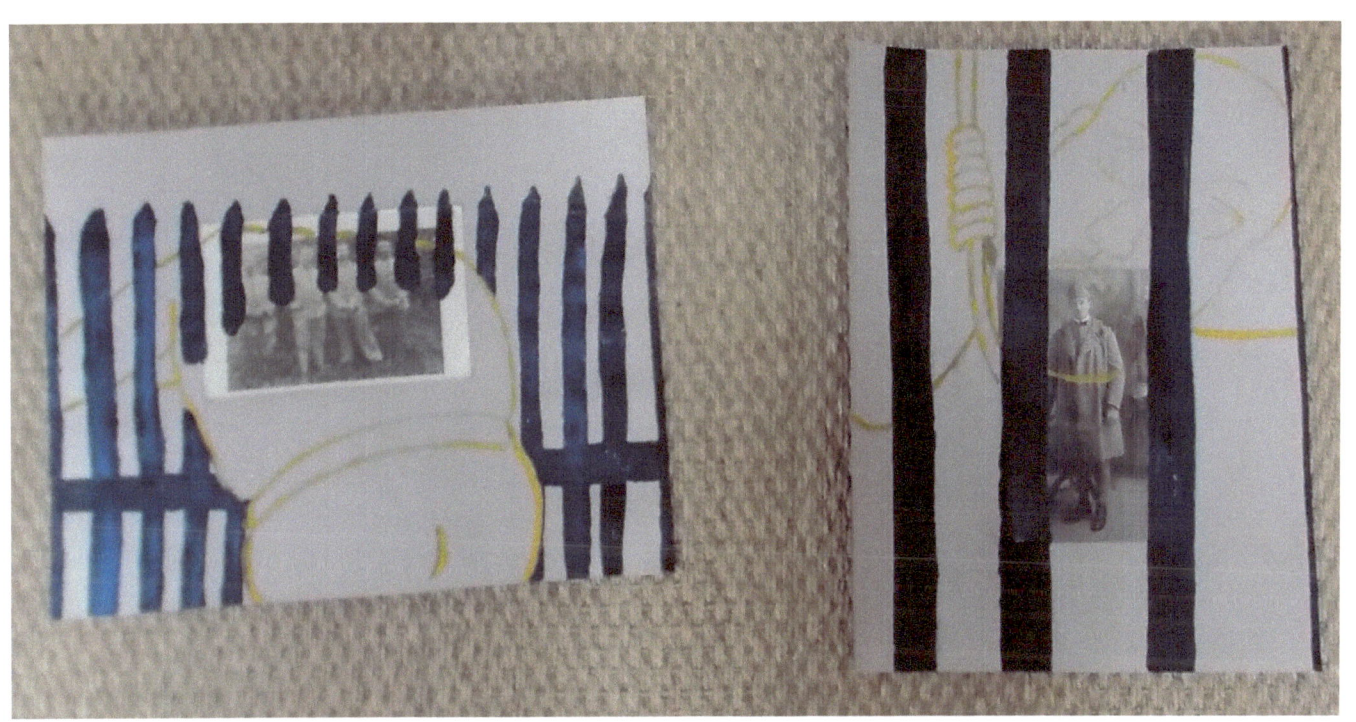

Left to right:

What Is The Point?; No Choice Hero.

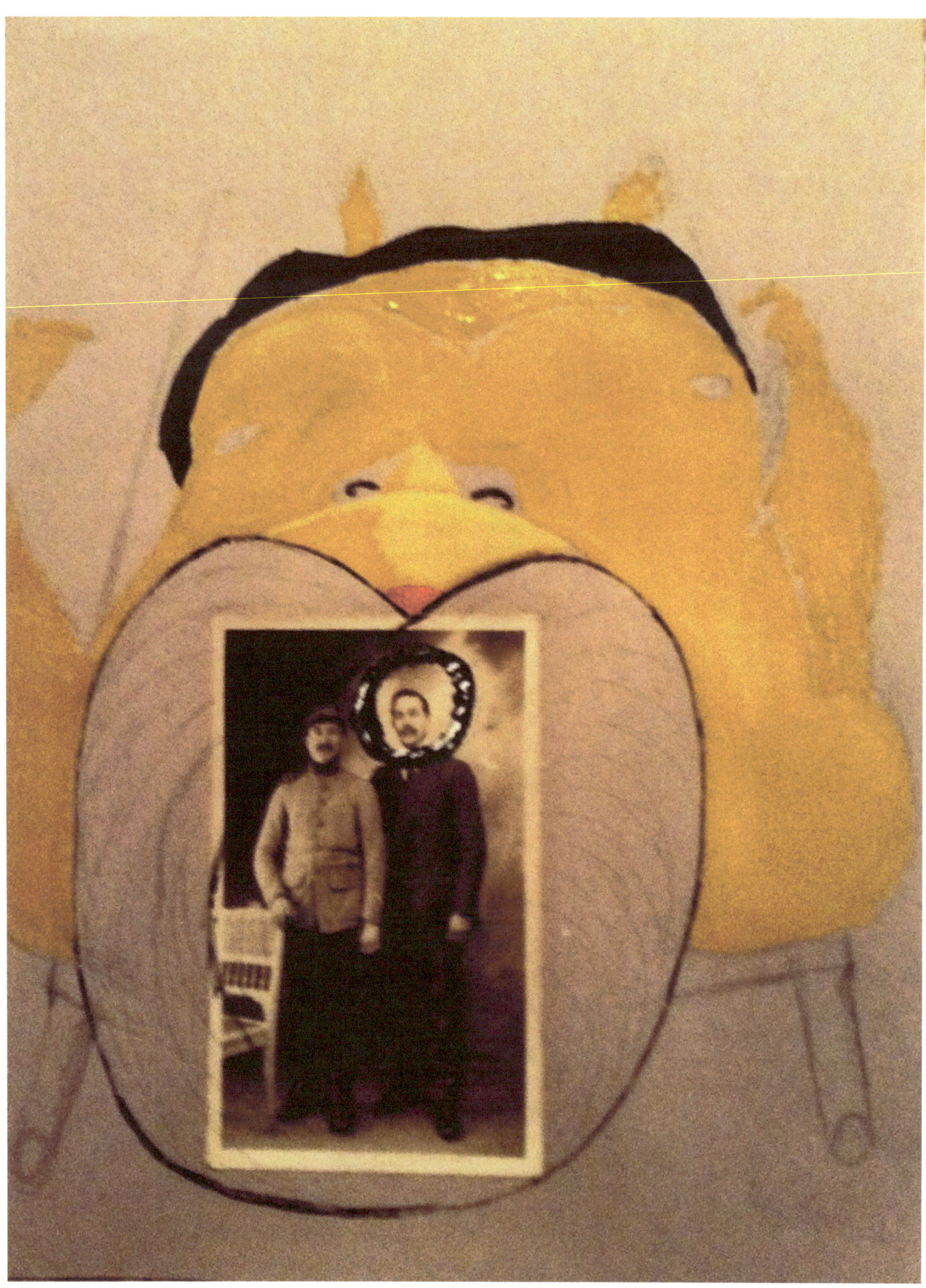

Falling.

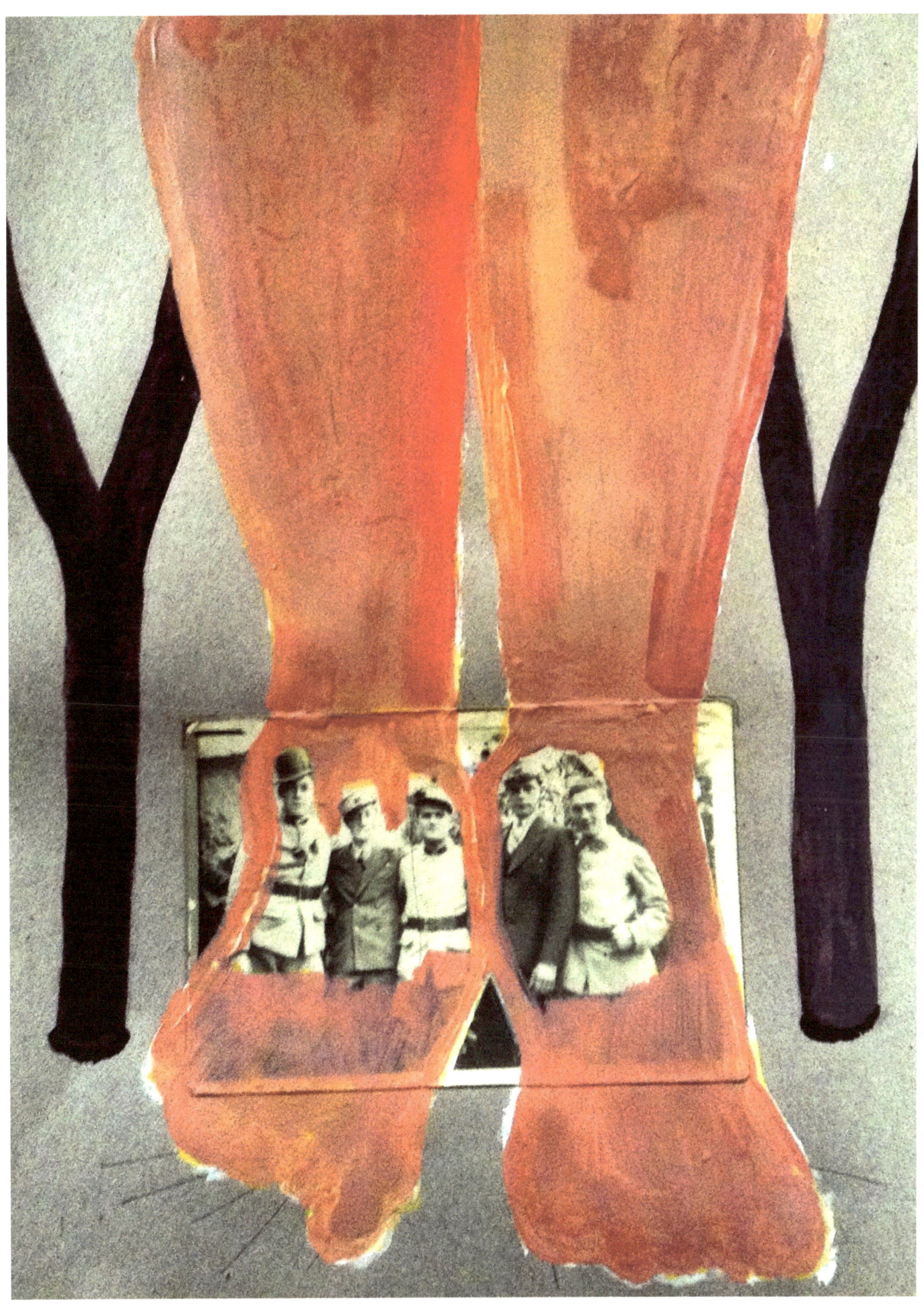

Grounding Props.

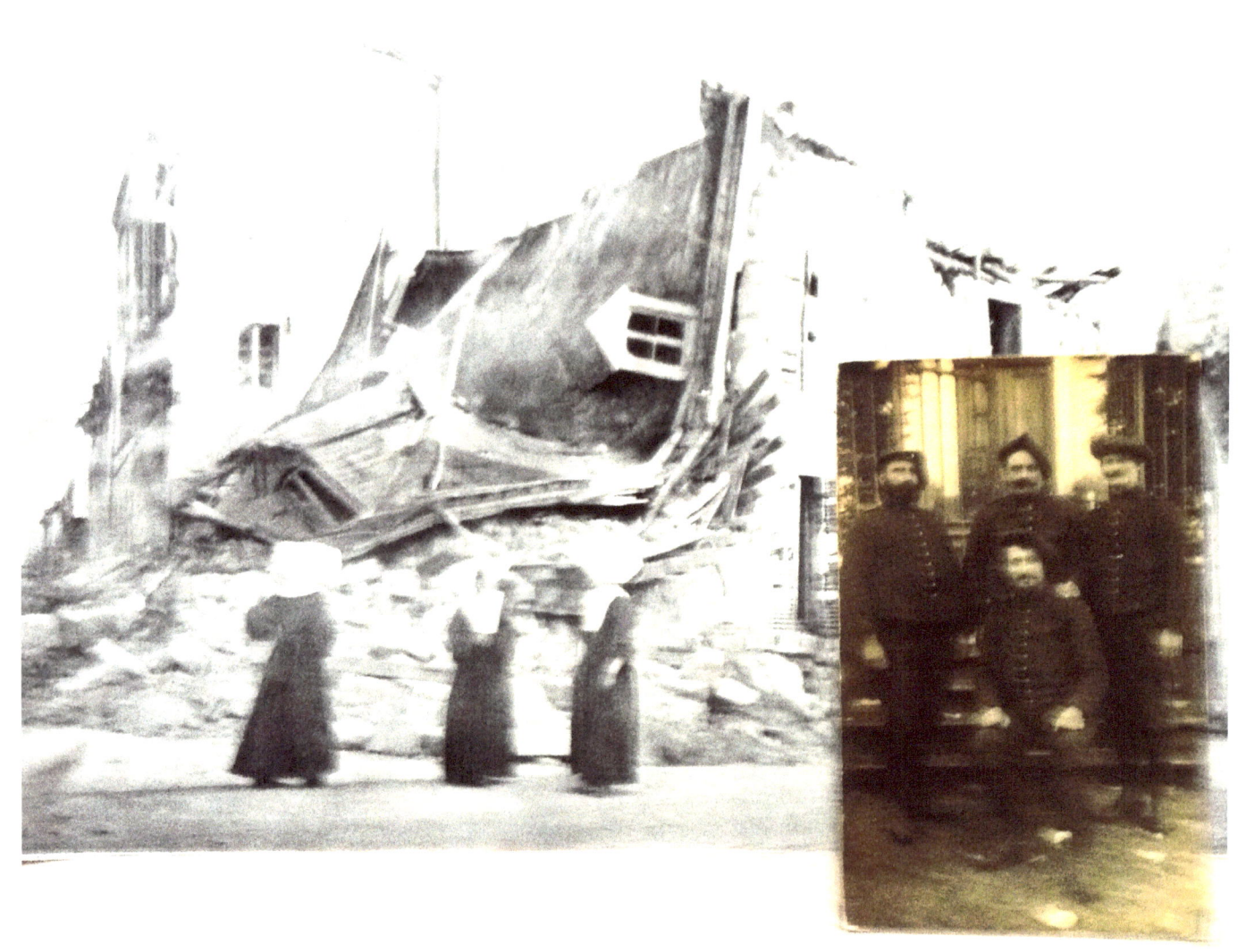

Ruined Bodies.

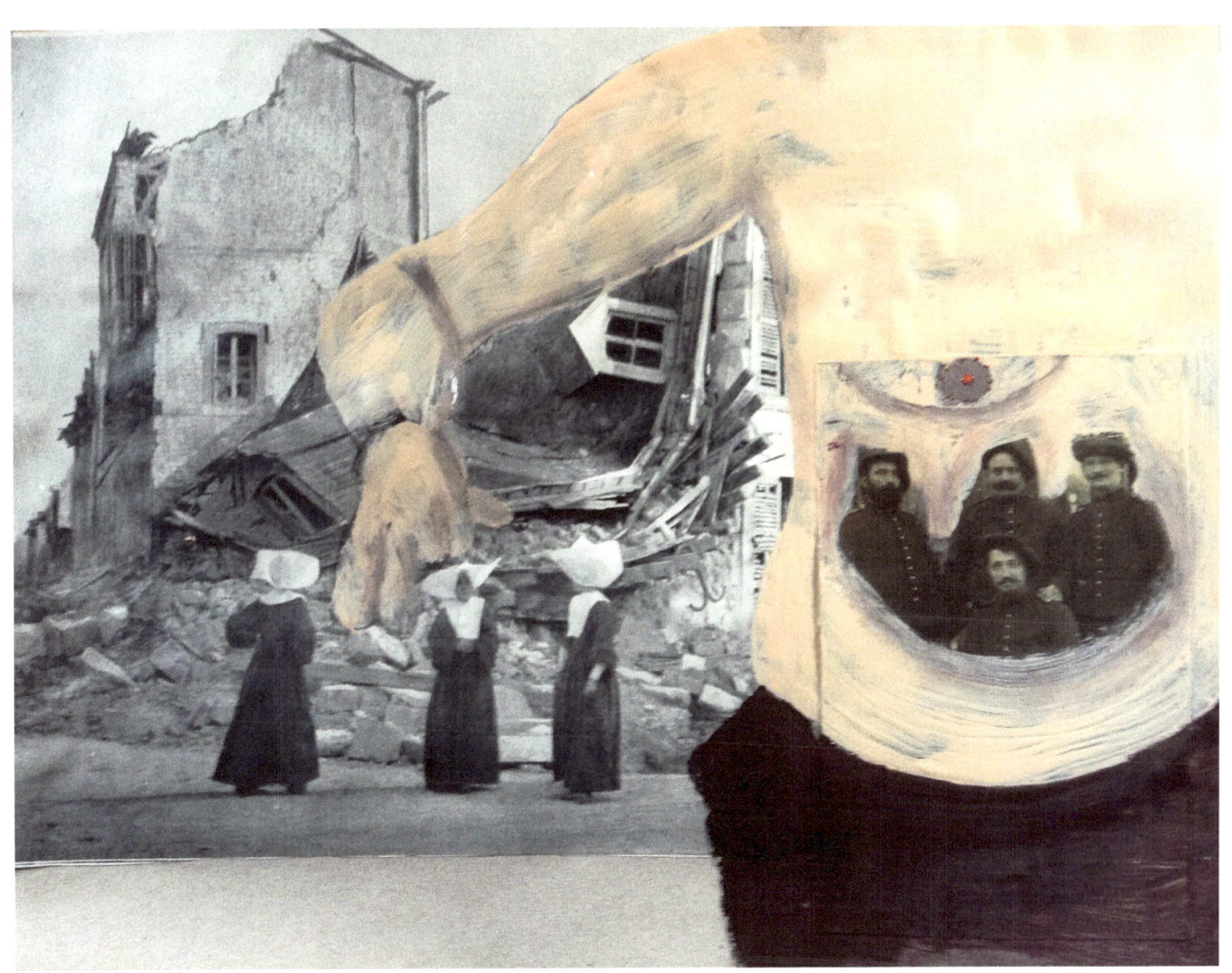

Ruined Bodies.

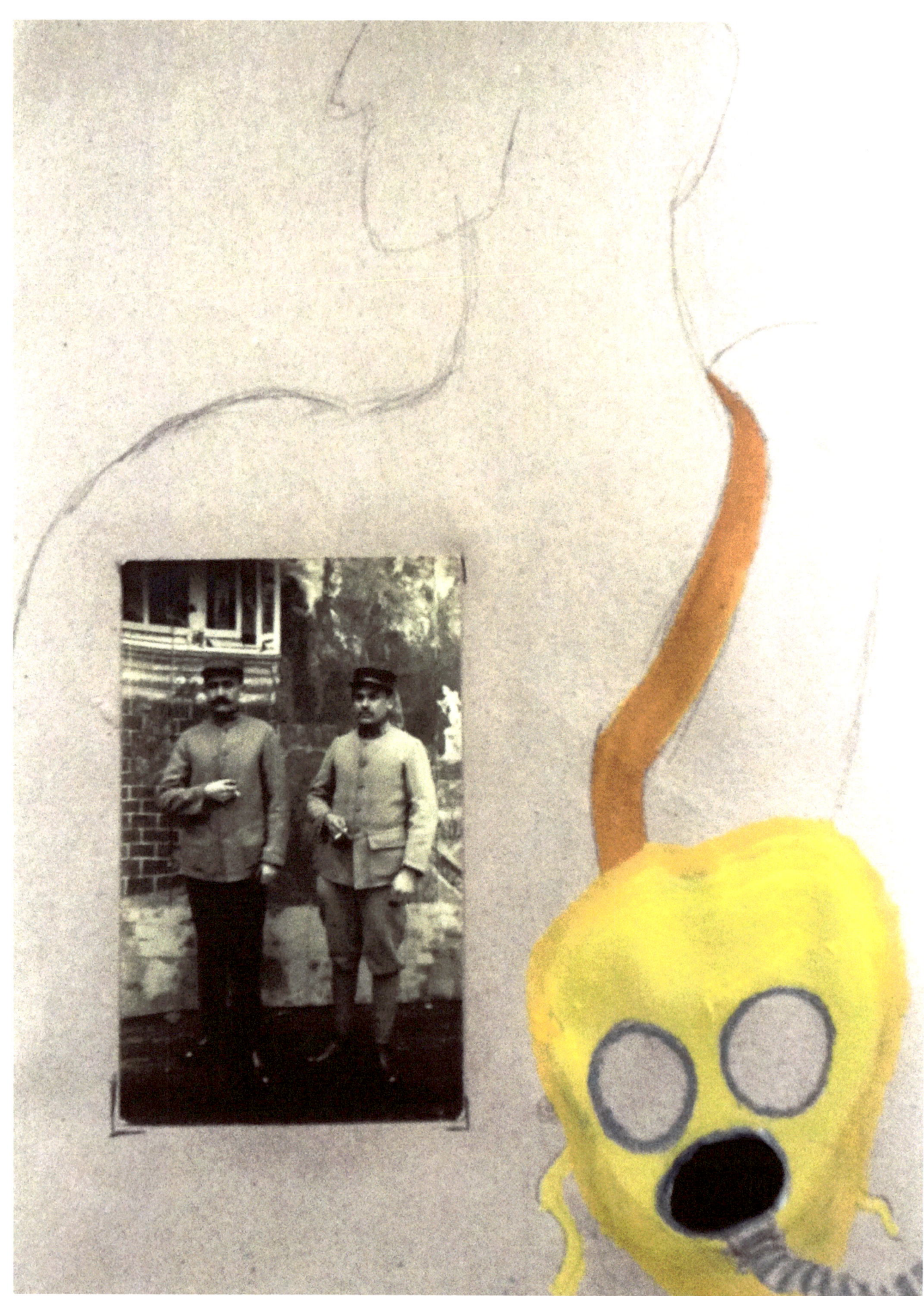

Exuding.

THE SOURCES.

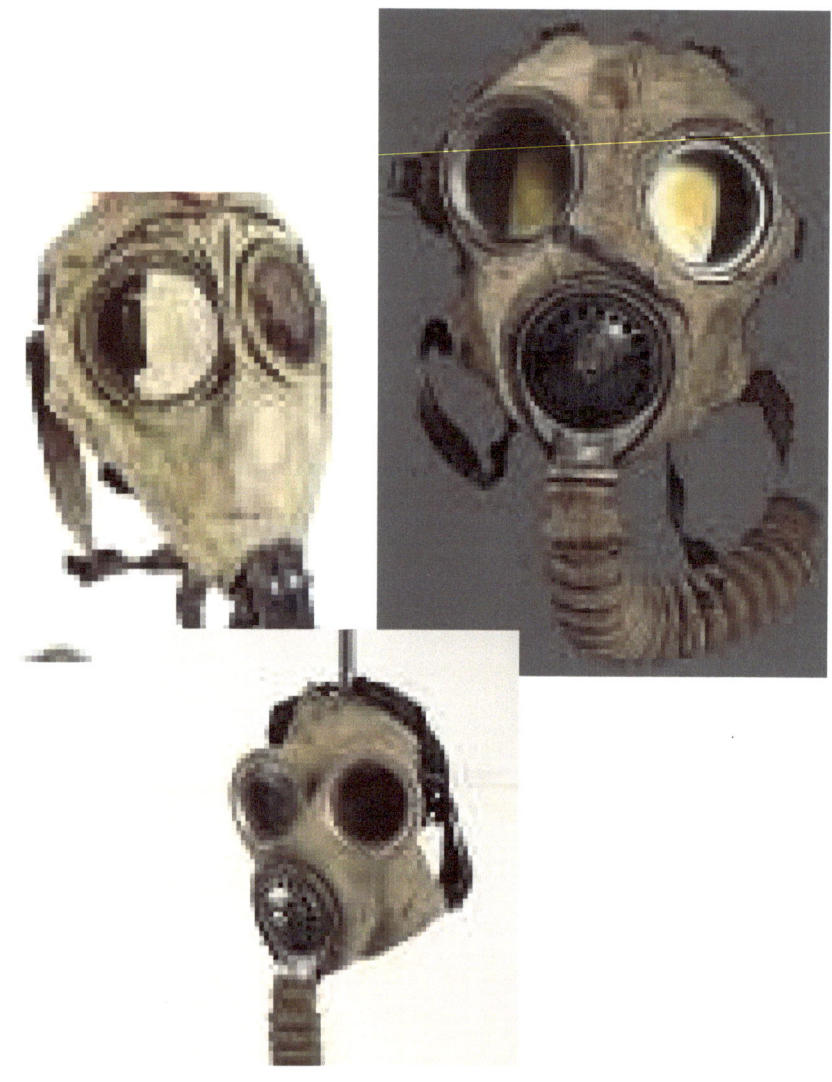

Exuding.

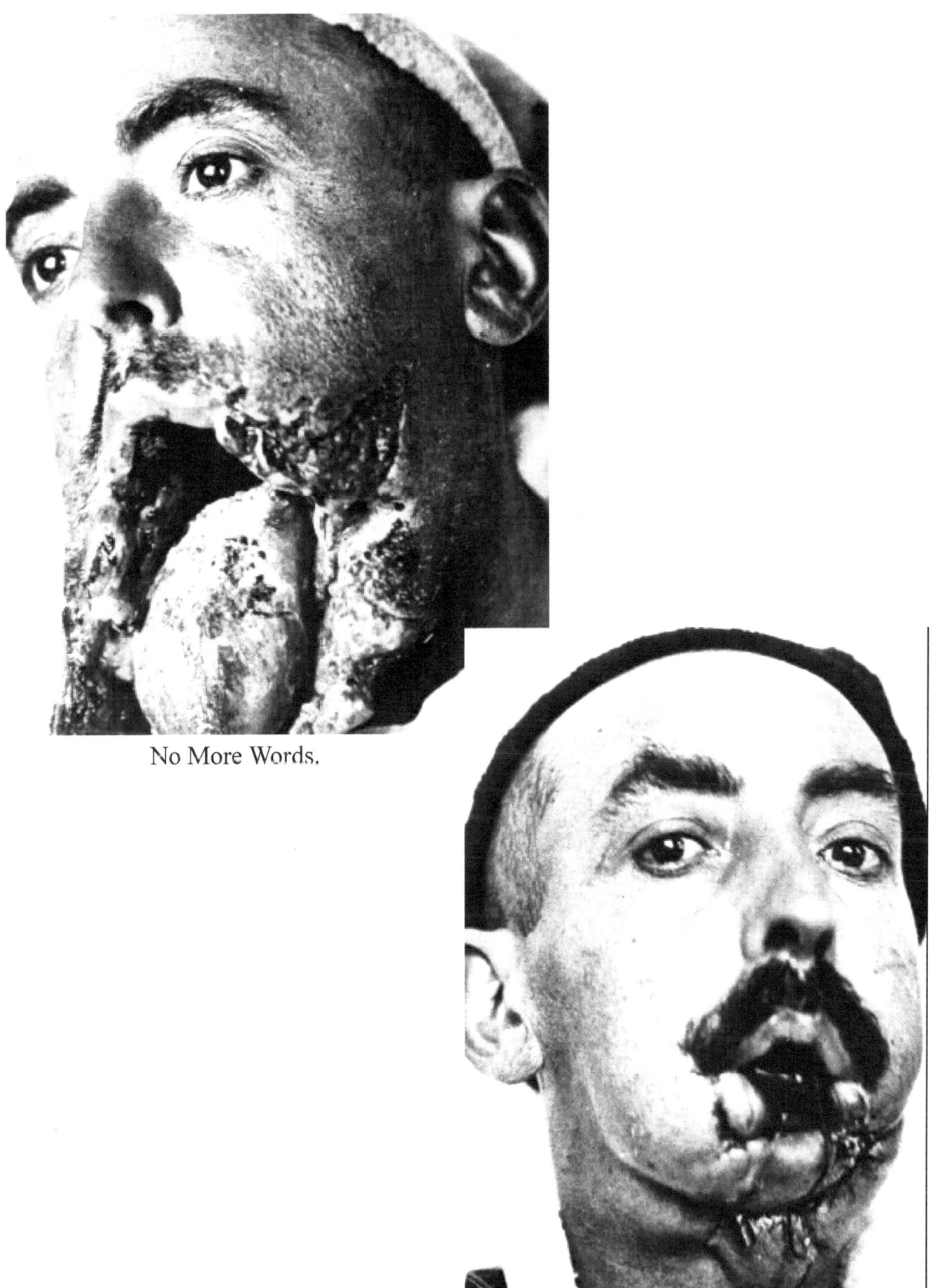

No More Words.

No More Words..

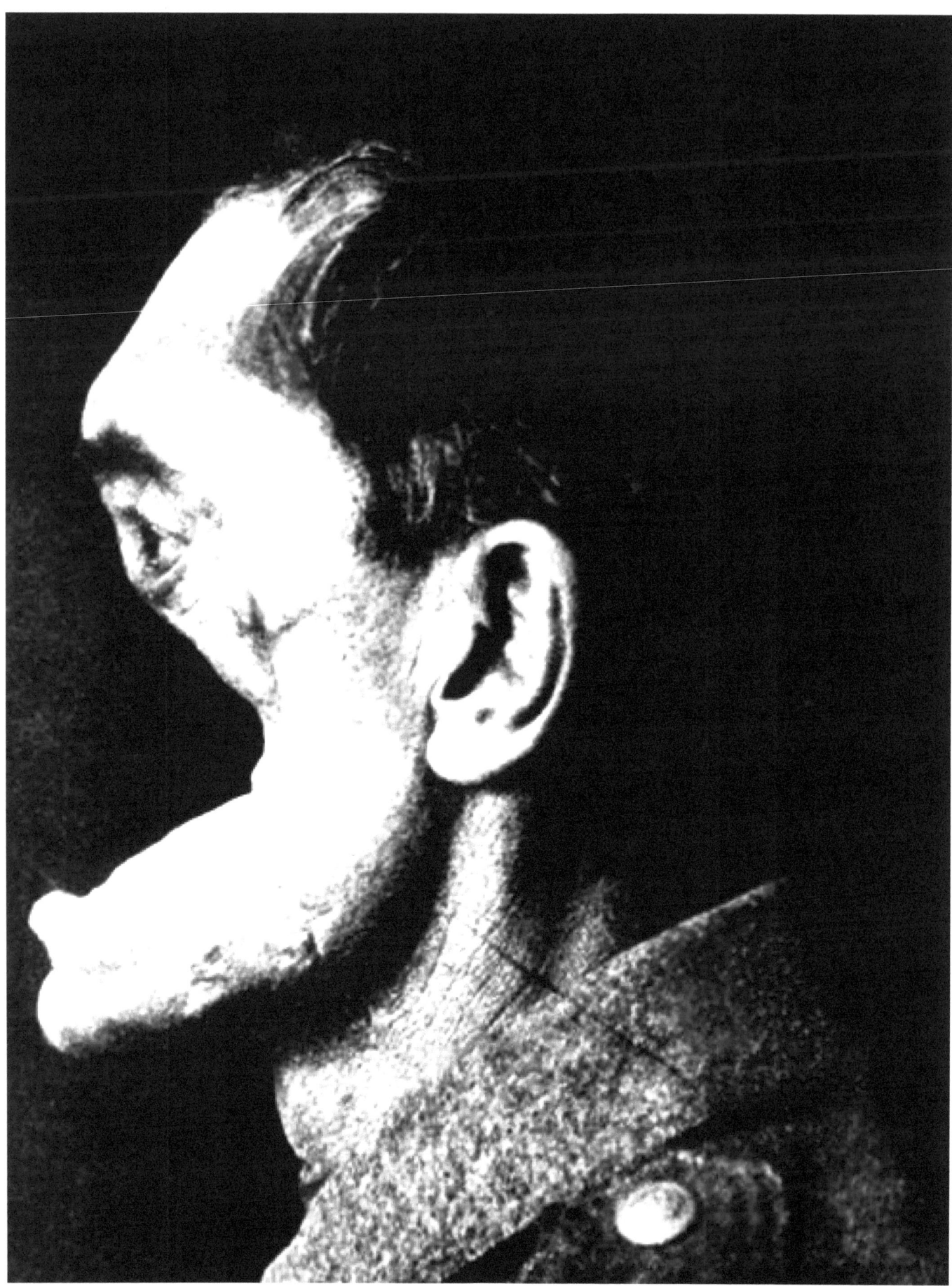

Hole -y War.

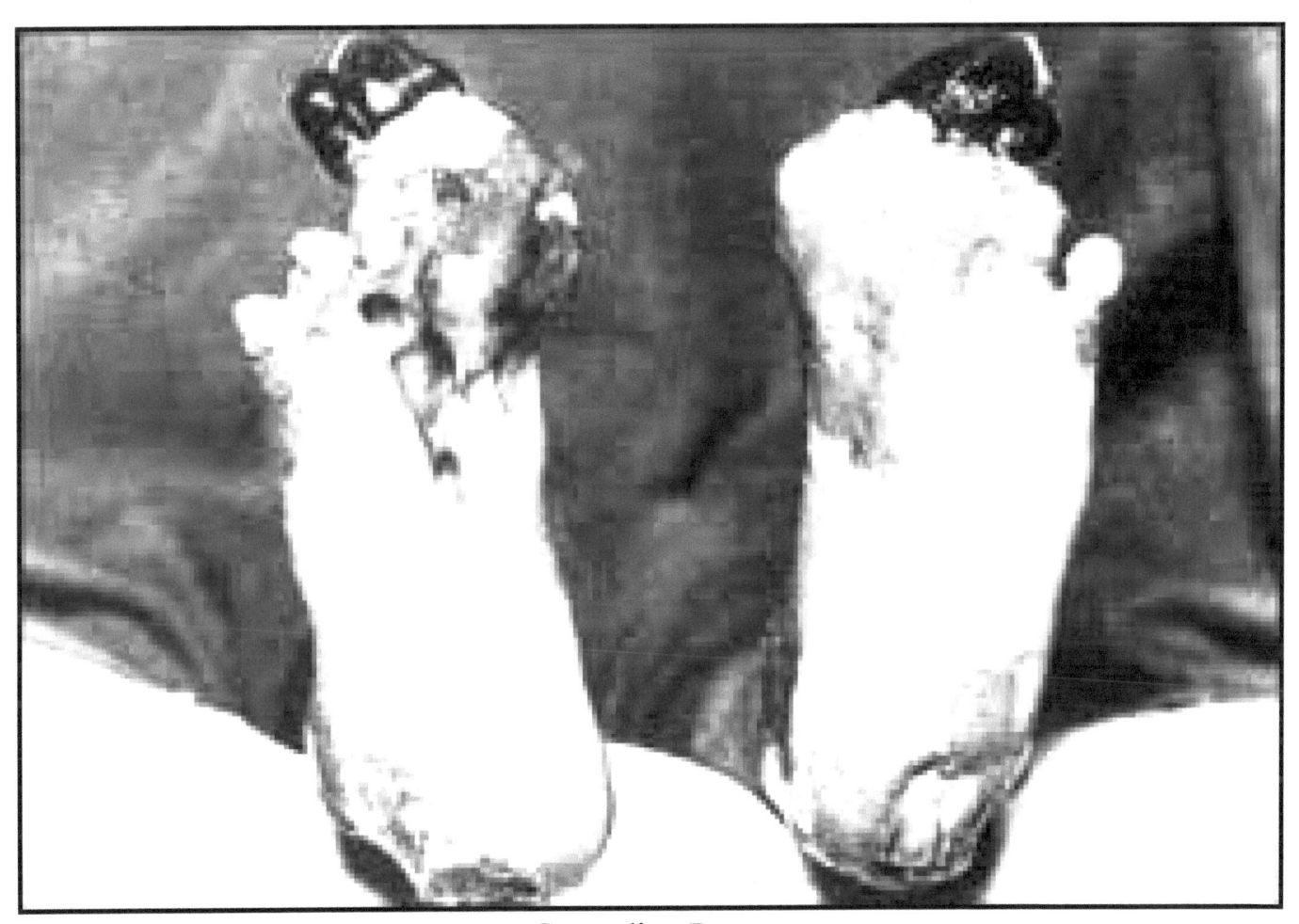

Grounding Props.

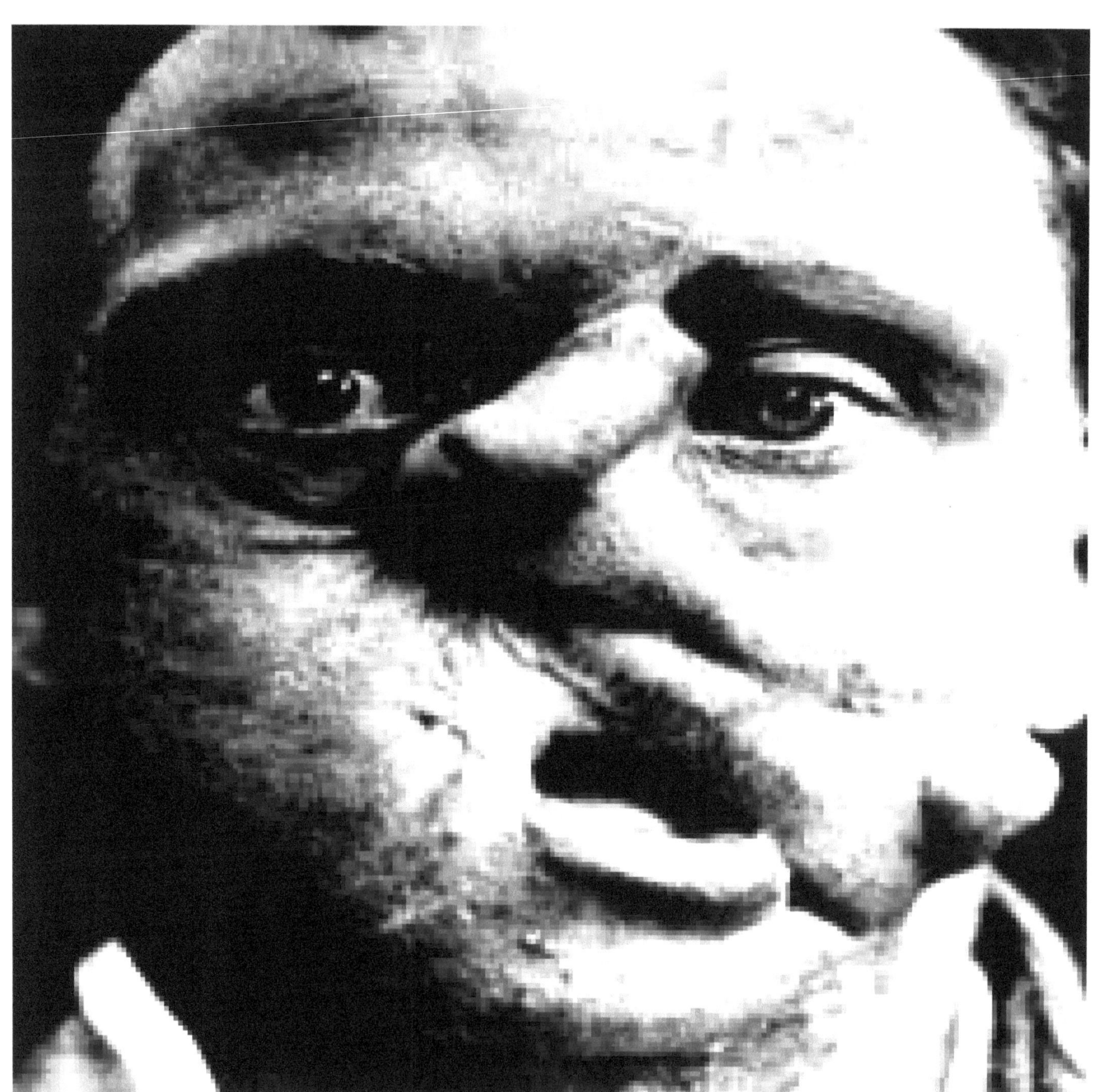

The Frustrations Of The Gourmand.

Future projects in this Pentad are:

Phase Three '*The Theatre of War*' (A book and paintings about the theatre groups formed in the WW1   Prisoner of War Camps (first image here) Exhibiting 2017.

Phase Four '*Gays in the Military*' (a book and paintings of homoeroticism and homosexuals in WW1) Exhibiting 2018.

Phase Five '*Out with a Bang!*', (a book and paintings exploring the irony of the feeble end of the war and the difficult lives experienced by the returning soldiers) Exhibiting 2019.

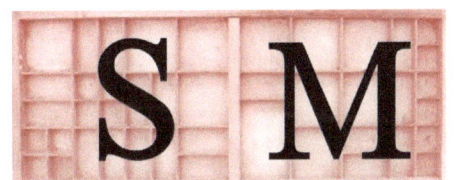

Sachet Mixte Publications.

www.sachetmxte.com

www.ingramcontent.com/pod-product-compliance
Lightning Source LLC
Chambersburg PA
CBHW040746200526
45159CB00023B/1754